Every Time I Go Home I Break Out In Relatives

Juliet Vandenburg

Every Time I Go Home I Break Out In Relatives

SYLVIA HARNEY

Wolgemuth & Hyatt, Publishers, Inc.
Brentwood, Tennessee

Wolgemuth & Hyatt, Publishers, Inc.
1749 Mallory Lane, Suite 110
Brentwood, Tennessee 37027

Library of Congress Cataloging-in-Publication Data

Harney, Sylvia.
    Every time I go home I break out in relatives / Sylvia Harney. —
1st ed.
       p. cm.
    ISBN 0-943497-60-4
    1. Family—Humor. 2. Family life—Humor. 3. Kinship—Humor.
I. Title. II. Title: Every time I go home I break out in relatives.
PN6231.F3H36 1990
306.85'0207—dc20   90-12937
                                        CIP

This book
is tenderly dedicated
to "The Family"—mine,
yours, and all the others in
this world who are faithfully
choosing to pass down
from one generation
to another the greatest legacy
of all—love.

My family has passed down
a few other things to me, but
I decided not to mention
them here.

CONTENTS

FOREWORD

(Confessions of a Literary Widower—Part Two)

It's quiet in the house. The soft green glow of Sylvia's computer screen stares blankly at me through a legion of fast food fingerprints and a few tear stains. The book is finished.

Just days ago this normally sunny, peaceful room, resembled a mix of Manned Space Flight Control at NASA and a certain government office just before the shredder was turned on.

Several months ago, I jokingly told a friend my wife was pregnant with her second book. I had no idea how startlingly close to the truth that remark was . . . and unlike the biological version, labor has lasted the entire gestation period.

Writing a humorous book on the family, or at least Sylvia's family, does not suffer from lack of material. Sifting through the antics of two or three generations is a lot like adding extra punch lines to the transcript of a congressional hearing and then condensing it to fit into the space of a short article in the *Reader's Digest*.

If your family is dull, boring, uninteresting and devoid of humor, you may have a hard time believing this book. At this writing Sylvia and I have been married thirteen years. In that relatively brief time, I have witnessed and in many cases experienced enough amazing things in this family to fill at least two installments of a Time-Life Book series. Truth is truly more amazing than fiction. Maybe she should have done this in a series. We could run a commercial on television. Get hooked up with Visa and Mastercard. Take orders on our own 800 number and have the UPS truck running in and out like Delta flights in the Atlanta Airport . . . oh, well, maybe next time.

I invite you to join Sylvia Harney on this exploration of the family. You may laugh some, you may cry, you may get an emotional elbow in the ribs or a shin kick under the table. You will think about your family life and find joy in remembering how it was, healing in remembering when it wasn't what it should have been, and hope in learning what it can be.

Things are returning to normal at our house. We are back on speaking terms with the dog, my socks all match again, and Sylvia has enrolled in a remedial cooking class.

Sincerely,
HANK

Dear Hank,

I dropped out of the cooking class. The cookbook didn't have any pictures in it!

Love,
SYLVIA

TO MY READER

Gentle laughter and tender truths go together like a hot dog and mustard. The gentle laughter lifts you up, and the tender truths burrow in and sit a spell.

Someone has said that laughter gives us a chuckle now and a smile two hours later and is a better pick-me-up than a morning cup of coffee. I made that up myself, but think about it. How often do you find yourself smiling two hours after your morning cup of coffee? But gentle laughter's different. It has no caffeine, and just the memory of it lasts most of a lifetime.

Often for each of us the tender truths come from our very personal learning experiences—and in many cases, the laughter comes from those same places.

So it is my hope that in sharing moments from my families—my childhood family, my present family, and families I have known and loved—that you will be able to discover your own treasures hidden among memories long passed over as unimportant, too difficult to remember, or lacking in permanent value. As is usually the case, some of our most prized treasures are tucked away where we'd least expect to find them—right there amidst the everyday tedium of life.

Just Thought You Might Like to Know

"Just because you have a great sense of humor is no reason to go on a vacation to test it!"

"Middle-child syndrome was first experienced by a third child who was forced to ride in the back seat without a window."

"When your child asks for a puppy, give the child a horse—or anything else too big to bring into the house."

"The mother who actually tries to save a 'stitch in time' is a type A personality."

"Contrary to what teenagers think, mothers are not contagious; teenagers cannot catch a foul disease from hugging one."

"The song, 'I've Got Tears in My Ears from Lyin' on My Back Cryin' over You' was written by a parent waiting for a teenager to come home from a date."

"If your washing machine comes with a ten-year warranty, it will blow up the day after it turns ten."

"If you live with an adolescent and feel a twinge in your hip, check your billfold; your money will be missing."

"The child who 'truly' has everything is the child whose parents love each other."

"There will be no sock sorting in heaven."

ACKNOWLEDGMENTS

I'm overwhelmingly thankful for my family—all of you: Momma and Daddy, my aunts and uncles, my zillions of delightful cousins, all my nephews down to the very least one—tiny baby Bill (who is only three months new to this family). I could be equally grateful for nieces, but we don't have any. Whose fault is that?

I'm grateful for all the people who are encouragers in my life. My husband, Hank, tops the list. This book was conceived and written during the most difficult time of my life (up to this point, that is). It was written, thrown in the trash, rewritten, prayed over, cried over, and finally completed only by God's tender grace (not to mention the fact that Hank refused to let me quit).

My deepest thanks and appreciation to Steve Hines, a marvelous writer and gifted editor who walked me through a very tough time. Thank you for believing I could do it and for pointing me in the right direction. You made me desire to keep on getting better at putting words together.

Thanks to all the wonderful people at Wolgemuth & Hyatt Publishers who know that I'm a little bit crazy but like me anyway. (It's sort of like family!) I am most thankful to your committment to quality and the highest standards possible.

I thank the Lord for the fact that we're all made in His image—even those people to whom we're related.

INTRODUCTION

I had finally reached the age of discovery. I was twelve, and I learned that twelve is too old to be a child but not old enough to qualify for anything else. I'd discovered boys and had just about decided not to look for anything else.

I discovered wearing stockings and that keeping the seams straight was just about as impossible as liking algebra. I discovered that my best friend's dime-store lipstick turned bright orange on me and was nigh unto impossible to wash off. It was "wash n' wear"; you could wash it until your lips cracked, but you'd still be wearing it when you went home from school—which was how my mother discovered I was wearing lipstick at school.

My twelfth year of life was to be the beginning of many lifelong discoveries. I began to discover what my family was all about. It began at a family reunion.

When you're twelve and have a serious case of self-consciousness to begin with, all it takes is a few pimples and a family reunion to make you believe every eye within a fifty-mile radius is zeroed in on you.

When you sit in a room full of relatives who haven't seen you in a year, you *know* what they're thinking. . . . *Well, if she's going through an ugly stage, it sure has stretched into a long one!*

3

When your braces stick out farther than your chest, you don't dare smile and draw attention to the fact. You just opt for keeping your mouth shut and grinning once in a while.

It was at a gathering like that, where all the aunts and uncles said, "Come here, and just let me look at you," that I learned something. I learned that if you stare at a grown-up relative long enough, if you refuse to talk, if you grin without opening your mouth, even a fairly self-confident adult will eventually turn the attention elsewhere. When you're "only" twelve you can get away with behavior like this. Your parents think you're weird, but you can still get away with it.

When I had tolerated all the being looked at I could bear, I retreated to the upstairs of my grandmother's house. I reached the upstairs landing just as another roar of laughter burst from the living room. "One of us children ought to go in there and tell those grown-ups to keep it down." A room full of adults who are related to each other can get away with more noise than children because there's no one to call them down.

My grandmother's house had its own peculiar smell, like a special cologne worn only by houses that have outlived at least one generation. Voices were coming from every room. I heard whispers and the creaking of the front porch swing. That would be my cousin Margaret Ann and that "young man" she'd brought with her. They didn't fool me one bit, even if I was only twelve. She introduced him as her "friend" somebody or other. I forgot his name, but I didn't forget how he looked at Margaret Ann. He was a bit flushed, and she didn't look one bit better.

My grandmother wouldn't be happy about people who weren't married to each other sitting too close in her swing, I thought as I pushed open the door to the room I secretly called my "treasure room." It was a semi-forbidden room rarely used for anything other than storing old worn-out pieces of life. It was a room that reeked of the past and always succeeded in carrying me away from the present.

An eight-foot-long wooden trunk-like chest lived in that room and called to me every time I visited my grandmother. Remnants of what I believed to be my grandmother's treasures lived inside that chest. And in the privacy of that dark, musty room I would bury myself in its contents for hours. There were beaded handbags smelling of fancy perfume; there was a pair of black high heels with bows on the toes; there were dresses and gowns, necklaces, earrings, and bracelets. I put them all on at once and clomped around that room in my grandmother's shoes.

Then the call to dinner would come ringing up the stairs, and I would hastily fold the clothes, re-move all the jewelry and the shoes, and place them lovingly back in the chest before reluctantly joining the rest of the family.

The dining room was always filled corner to cor-ner with people and the table covered end to end with food. Tiny children squirmed their way through a sea of grown-up legs to stand eye level with the turkey, ham, and homemade rolls. Numerous sets of tiny fingers came to rest on the edge of the bountiful table in eager anticipation of grabbing the first edible morsel within reach as soon as the blessing ended.

Then, for the first time all day, there would be silence as my daddy led us in the blessing. He blessed everything from the Lord Himself to His wonderful day to the cooks who had prepared the meal we were about to eat. Then he always said, "And thank you, Lord, for family and loved ones, in Jesus' name, Amen."

That was 1959. I'm obviously not twelve anymore, and except for rare and occasional flare-ups, I no longer have pimples. My cousin Margaret Ann married "what's his name," and we've been calling him Uncle Pete for years now. So I guess that must be his name. They have children who are grown and one who has married. My Aunt JuJu and Momma still laugh louder than anybody else. There are about thirty times more people in the family now than there were back then, so the general noise level has reached an all-time high when we get together. And my Grandmother Grigsby is no longer with us.

The family got together and divided up her possessions when she died. No one knew about my relationship with the chest in the upstairs room, and I don't know what happened to it. But two of her dresses hang in my closet, and some of her brooches live in a small box in my bureau drawer. They are tiny remnants of the contents of that wonderful chest.

The chest is gone, but my memories are as fresh as the day before yesterday. Because I'm not twelve anymore, I now know that the contents of my grandmother's chest were not her treasures at all. Nor was her house or furniture listed among her valuables. The people who filled those rooms were her timeless treasures. It was the laughter cascading off the walls, the children running in the front door and out the back with some parent hot on their trail yelling, "Stop that running in and out, do you hear me? It's either *in* or *out*. Pick one!" Those were her treasures.

Now, I understand why Mother Grigsby's living room was wall-to-wall with two big sofas and umpteen unmatched chairs in those later years. It was because decor no longer mattered; the fellowship of people sitting around talking did matter, and the more the merrier. So her treasures were people whose lives were woven together by the mysterious birthing process that creates families.

Her treasures were wrapped up in the noise of relatives smacking their knees with laughter as a familiar story received yet another telling. In reality, without even realizing it, my grandmother did pass her treasures on to me. I'm fortunate to know what my treasures are before it's too late. Because where our treasures are our hearts will be.

This book is committed to helping all of us look for and find the joy, the humor, the treasures hidden in the ordinary, everyday life.

1

MY TREASURES
ARE LOCKED
IN THE TRUNK
OF MY FAMILY TREE
(Family Heritage)

When I was eight I thought my family tree was something that lived in the front of my granddad's Bible. There were lines drawn out like a real tree with branches going off in every direction. It had names of people I'd never heard of and people I'd never met. What worried me was that my name wasn't on it yet and that if it had been, my branch would have extended off the page way up there—and I'm afraid of heights.

I remember wondering what you had to do to get a family tree. Later I found out all you had to do was be born and presto! You popped out somewhere as another branch. The first time I read in the Bible about all those "who begat whoms," I thought all that begatting sounded like they were doing something awful to each other. But I was only seven or eight at the time. I was afraid there might be some begatting going on in my family that I didn't know about. When I learned that begat meant somebody had married and had a family, I was so relieved.

Now I'm married and have a family.

My family resembles the Brady bunch. Hold it! Before you throw this book to the floor and set fire to it, read on. My husband just looked over my shoulder and choked on his coffee. Okay, my family doesn't resemble the Brady bunch, but some of us *are*

11

blond! When I got married I thought my family would be a *little* like the Brady bunch. The children would all be manageable and clean. I would live in a self-cleaning house with a live-in maid who never had anything to do. The grass would be perpetually green but would never grow. And the father would go around dressed up, smelling nice, and pretending that he had to go to work. Does that sound like reality to you?

I did believe that if and when I had children, they would show me the courtesy of dressing to please me and would eat things that fell into at least one of the four basic food groups. I did get a self-cleaning house—I clean it myself. I did not know that I would forever be picking up stuff somebody else just threw down. I did not know that mold and mildew would inhabit the land and that teenage boys don't care if they smell like ode-to-locker room. I did not know that children have no use for closets except in the case of dire emergencies. (One of our boys used his closet to conceal a live guinea pig for close to three weeks before the fragrance gave it away.)

I had absolutely no clue that once a year, at tax time, a normally sane husband would go around as if he were preparing for a role in the remake of *It's a Mad, Mad, Mad, Mad World* and that he would insist we were using too much bathroom tissue. No one told me that there is some kind of written rule that during the busiest weeks of your life, the washing machine will throw a terminal fit and refuse to agitate, spin, or drain. I did not know it was possible for the dishwasher door to fly open in mid-cycle, or that lettuce will freeze in the bottom of the refrigerator, or that ice cream will never freeze no matter where you put it.

I did not know that sheets refuse to stay on the mattress, or that if you leave wet clothes in the washing machine for twenty-four hours, they develop some kind of unidentifiable mold and have to be rewashed. I believed everything I read—like labels that said "childproof," "wrinkle-resistant," "waterproof," and "do not remove under penalty of law." The first time one of the children took it upon himself to test the law by removing that tag, the cat grabbed it and ate it. For weeks I looked for myself on the FBI's ten-most-wanted list.

I was honestly guilty of believing that my childhood family would always understand me, would always be thinking about me, and would send me little cards on my birthday telling me how wonderful I am.

I did get something from one of my brothers just this year—a picture of a man eight hundred pounds overweight with a caption that reads, "I guess I just never ate enough oat bran when I was growing up." It was such an encouragement to me. It was also unsigned, but I *know* where it came from and who sent it. Just staying in touch with all these people is a challenge. My mother won't call me because she has an unnatural fear of answering devices, and when Daddy calls he hangs up on me while I'm in the middle of a sentence. My momma collects absolutely everything, and Daddy throws everything away. He loves to dig holes in the ground and to take equipment apart so my brothers will have something to "fix" when they go see him.

If you could sit down long enough to bring to mind all the little surprises you've encountered in your family, by the time you completed the list, you'd be too old to get up again.

You May Not Be the Bradys, But You Do Have a Bunch

Not long after you get married, you begin to think about enlarging your family. I, for one, believe that a couple can make up a family, that two people can be a complete unit all by themselves, because some people aren't able to have children or to adopt. But what most of us think about when we hear the word *family* is a couple of married adults and some offspring.

So, soon after you get married you begin to daydream about beginning your own little bunch. The dream usually involves what I heard one young lady describe as pushing a tiny baby around in a cute little wicker baby buggy. Cars would pass and honk; people would open doors for you, stop, bend over the carriage, go "ooh and aah," and say, "Isn't he cute?" Then you'd have to tell them that "he" is a "she" (and you wonder what kind of an idiot can't tell a boy from a girl). It's like the story of a little boy who was sitting outside with his new pet. A neighbor walked by and said, "Oh, how cute. Is it a boy or a girl?" The little boy looked at her as if she'd lost her mind and said, "It's a puppy!"

So off you go pushing your beginning of a bunch blissfully down life's never-ending sidewalk.

I have to admit that sounds so good it could almost make me want to run out and find some babies in a buggy that need someone to push them through life. Then I realize I'm still woozy from the last child we lovingly nudged and prodded through life and that it isn't over yet.

Reality comes crashing in on us sooner than we ever expect it and long before it is invited. Every young mother quickly finds out exactly how long you can get away with pushing a baby around in a carriage—about several minutes would be my guess—before something needs to be changed, fed, or fixed. The truth is, it's just hard to keep a good baby down when the rest of us are walking around on two legs. It isn't long before they decide to try out their own legs. When they do, the action is just beginning. And the baby buggy goes into storage along with most of our preconceived notions about family life. When this same little person reaches the age of two and becomes the master of special effects, we have an opportunity to test our endurance and to discover if we have a sense of humor.

When we get married, we think we know everything. Then by the time we realize we don't know anything, we're almost too busy to do anything about it. This is where the concept of learning by experience comes from, and if we're very lucky, we never get too old or too experienced to keep on learning as we go along.

A Minor Collision—Major Change

A family begins sometime after two people who are total opposites bump into each other and turn around to see what hit them. This is what you can honestly call a minor collision and the beginning of major change. By the time these two people begin to figure out what hit them, they will have been married for ten years and will have a house payment that is probably too big, one car that is too small, and two children at home scuffling over whether to watch "Mr. Rogers" or "Davy Crockett" reruns. One child gags at the slightest suggestion of consuming green vegetables, and one eats so much he does his homework by the light in the refrigerator.

A family is organized chaos. This is a fact we don't consider while we're still dazed from the lovely collision of bumping into the love of our lives. The chaos really gets under way the day we begin to shop at unusual stores named "Babies R Us," or something like that, and all our dreams look like something from a Beatrix Potter book. Next, for no apparent reason that you can put your finger on, you're fighting the urge to sew yellow ruffles on your husband's undershirts. Or if you're a man, you go out and buy a football for a person who would rather have a pacifier.

My sister and her husband of three years have just been introduced to organized chaos. She called recently sounding like someone who had just won a million dollars in the *Reader's Digest* sweepstakes. She was so out of breath that I thought she needed medical attention. She's having her first baby.

She said, "Sissy, how'd you like to go see USA Baby?"

When I asked her where it was playing, there was a long pause. She waited for me to get over the misconception that I was funny and charged right on.

She spent three minutes trying to tell me how excited her husband was over selecting the ribbons for the bumper pads in the baby bed. I bet he was. The last pads he had anything to do with were the ones under his football uniform.

The last time I was with her, she wanted me to notice how her hips had spread out. I've never heard of a woman being excited about that before. (She'll be even more excited when she finds out that they don't go back after the baby comes.)

This is just the beginning of all the changes a tiny baby brings about in a couple's life. Babies have a lot of power, and it begins prenatally. I've never had a big decision to make over the issue of when life begins. A baby is a baby, and that's all there is to it. Can you imagine a woman calling up her husband after her pregnancy test comes up positive and saying, "Honey, guess what? We have a fetus. . . . Aren't you excited?" Of course not. She says, "Honey, we're going to have a baby!" And they begin to celebrate this baby because from the beginning it is understood to be the miracle of life.

This miracle of life caused me to drive all over town looking at baby beds during a time when my sister didn't even come close to looking as if she was expecting a baby. We started being excited over this new life long before there was outward evidence of its existence. This baby's been talked to, serenaded, and patted—and no one's even seen it yet.

Your body temporarily becomes public property when you announce you are going to have a baby. Total strangers slow down when you pass, give you these lopsided, goofy grins, and then move on.

One day my husband walked up to my sister, cupped his hands over her tummy, and said, "Hi, this is your Uncle Hank. How's everything going in there?" I quickly glanced at my sister. She grinned and said, "This baby just loves it when people talk to him." You can see that her introduction to chaos is well under way. Of course, we said that at their wedding too, but actually their chaos began when they bumped into each other on a sidewalk of their college campus years earlier and then turned around to see what hit them. They haven't figured it out yet.

Who Are These People?

It took some good ol'-fashioned nerve on my part when it came time to take the special someone in my life home to meet my family. When you take someone home to meet your relatives, you usually say it like this: "I'm taking him home to meet 'the' family." "The" family is always the only family in the world with the power to affect the rest of your life.

When I met the man who is now my husband, he was the epitome of total confidence and self-assurance. Then I took him home to meet "the" family. My family at that time was composed of six people who at just about any given moment acted as if they were auditioning for some kind of wild family game show. All six of them thought they were the funniest people since Johnny Carson. My husband says it wasn't on his list of fun activities to face a group of people all related to each other and snapping off one liners faster than you can say "Cracklin' Oat Bran."

To hear him tell it now, you'd think I dragged him out back to face a firing squad.

When we walked into the room to meet all those people, they were lined up around the room with their arms folded across their chests and deadpan looks on their faces. One of my brothers said to anyone who was listening, "He's big, isn't he?" The other brother said, "Yeah. Ugly too!" My mother kind of sniffed and said, "He has hair on his face." My dad said, "It's looking like it might turn cold." (It was the middle of July.) I kept expecting someone with John Wayne's voice to step out and say, "All right, big fella, tell us whatcha got on yer mind besides hair." That was when my sister pointed to me and said, "She's not easy to live with, you know." Then she proceeded to drag out the family photo album containing all the pictures of me before I blossomed into a human being. She held up the only picture in which I had a full-blown case of acne and said, "This is what she looks like with no makeup."

If her motive was to keep me all to herself, it didn't work. True love gives us the ability to overlook a lot of bumps—including acne. My husband thought the family was funny. I thought they were obnoxious. We were both right. That first meeting let me know that the man I wanted to marry could hold his own in this family, and that was very important to me. He's been holding his own ever since.

Bringing someone new into a family is the equivalent of opening the entire closet that houses Pandora's box. All the stuff you never wanted a living soul to know, see, or hear comes tumbling out. If there happens to be a storyteller in the bunch, he seizes both the opportunity and any available ears. He begins mouthing off stories about as exciting as listening to water drip.

You can no more skip this introduction to the family than you can decide going through puberty is a waste of time and jump straight into being eighteen. This is "Introduction to Family 101" at its best, and I don't recommend graduation into marriage without it.

After this initial meeting between my family and my husband-to-be, I thought there was probably nothing else they could possibly do to surprise him. I was wrong. I forgot about Christmas.

Sneak Up on 'Em And Take 'Em by Surprise

Some families have wonderful traditions at Christmas. They cook certain dishes; they wear special clothes; they sit around the Christmas tree sipping hot cider. Some of those families even talk to each other.

We have a tradition at Christmas. The first year that a new daughter- or son-in-law is "in" the family, the initiate receives a very special gift from the family. When my husband's first Christmas rolled around, he began unwrapping a lovely package. He pulled off the box top and lifted out the better half of a shirt that had been used for waxing furniture in a previous life. He sat there holding up that nasty half a shirt while the rest of us bent double in laughter.

He waited patiently for the laughter to die down. Then he turned to everyone in general and said, "I just want to know one thing. How long do I have to be in this family before I get the other half of this shirt?" You could say he passed the family exam with flying colors. He also passed along the shirt the next year.

My sister-in-law received a flannel gown with holes big enough to pass a volleyball through. She, too, passed along the lovely gown to an unsuspecting person the next year. No one seems to know what finally happened to that gown. I secretly suspect that another sister-in-law is using it.

Most of those bogus presents eventually disappear, but the laughter and fun will be with us forever.

You Get Your Spouse—Family and All

When you marry someone, you marry that person family and all. That's what everyone always told me. And just like you . . . I didn't believe a word of it when I married. But it's true. We marry them family and all. The ones we know, the ones we've never laid eyes on, the ones we like, the ones we, well, it's a little like one of my favorite stories from one of my hometowns.

An older couple in that small town got married after a lifetime of singleness. Ruby was a fiercely independent rural woman. She'd lived all of her sixty-some-odd—in fact, mostly odd—years making her own decisions with little or no outside interference from anyone, especially from anyone of the male persuasion. So it almost goes without saying that her marriage to Abe caused a sleepy town to wake up for a few days. Tongues got loose and started wagging, eyebrows were going up and down, and a few heads shook.

The ink on their marriage license was barely dry when the trouble began. Abe sold Ruby's hog. Not only did he sell her hog without asking her, he sold it without telling her. When Ruby discovered the missing hog, she had her new husband arrested. When Abe was brought before the judge, the judge said, "Abe, did you sell Ruby's hog?"

"Yessir," said Abe.

"Abe, when you married Ruby, did you know she had a hog?"

"Yessir," said Abe. "I knew she had a hog."

"Well, Abe, if you knew it was Ruby's hog, then why did you sell it?" the judge questioned.

"Well, Judge, it's like this. When I married Ruby, I married her hog and all!"

"Case dismissed," said the judge.

Now please refrain from attempting to draw any life-changing conclusions from this little story, for I fear there are none. It's just that when you get married, you do sort of unknowingly marry your spouse family and all. In this case, Ruby's *all* was her hog.

This is why being in a family can get complicated. Suddenly you have a spouse and another family to get to know. It's probably easier to back over your own foot while driving your car than to marry an entire family, but marrying a family is a lot more fun.

The Big Bang and Momma

Have you noticed that men have a fondness for being around big, loud noises, and women have a fondness for getting away from them?

The first few months after I married, I tried to plan my trips home so that everyone would be there at the same time. I wanted my husband to get to know this family he had married. Then the Fourth of July rolled around. Both my brothers have always had an attraction to loud noises, so this holiday is one of their favorites. They made a giant firecracker with black powder, stuffed it into a bathroom tissue roll, then buried it in the woods out back. They made one huge mistake. They forgot to warn Momma. When that thing went off Momma jumped high enough flat-footed to break a world record. My sister-in-law was in the bathroom at the time, and I don't have to tell you what she thought. In unison, four women went stomping out to the backwoods with our hands on our hips ready to say what was on our minds.

What we found were four grown men, my new husband included, all bent over the hole in the ground and grinning like a bunch of pyromaniacs. We could see how much pleasure our distress was bringing them, so we promptly stomped back into the house.

Momma muttered something about wondering how they would like to eat dirt for dinner, and the rest of us never said a word. I later remembered that we just weren't old enough to say what was really on our minds and get away with it. I was first exposed to this theory when my oldest brother brought his fiancée home while our maternal grandmother was making one of her three-month visits. My brother came waltzing into the living room with his arm around his girl. My grandmother took one quick look and whapped him on the arm with a rolled-up newspaper and said, "You get your hands off that girl this minute!"

He said, "Aw, Mother Grigsby, we'll be saying our nuptials soon."

She said, "I don't care if you can recite the Gettysburg Address, you get your hands off that girl!"

He did.

My husband says that the only thing greater than an older woman's age is her ability to speak what's on her mind and get away with it. My grandmother had reached that age, and I'm kind of looking forward to it myself.

I met another woman who looked as if she had reached that age. I saw a story in her face and went after it. "What kind of family did you think you would have when you married?" I asked her.

Without a hairbreadth of a pause she said, "A 'small' one."

"What happened?" I asked.

"Eight children, that's what happened!" she responded.

Well, that wasn't exactly what happened, I thought. But if she hadn't figured it out by then, she probably never would.

It did explain why she was wearing an old worn-out diaper as a neck scarf.

Meeting this woman reminded me of all the many times my parents went the extra mile for us. It reminded me that families do not fall into the "convenient" category. I'm fairly certain that most of us would not be around if our parents had waited until we were convenient. If you're looking for convenience, try a frozen dinner or McDonald's, but you'll get a lot more satisfaction from your family—especially if you can love them as they are, always desiring the best for them and never giving up when they let you down. My extended family goes on for about three thousand miles and several states. We have a relative behind every bush except George! And there's a story on the tip of every tongue. If I'm fortunate enough to live another forty years, I'll never come close to running out of stories.

2

---

*IF LOVE
MAKES THE WORLD
GO 'ROUND,
IT'S LAUGHTER
THAT KEEPS US
FROM GETTING DIZZY
(Learning to Laugh and Live)*

M_y family believes that laughter is just as important as eating right and exercising. I'd rather laugh than exercise anyway. A man came up to me at the close of a speaking engagement and asked me how he could give his wife a sense of humor: "She needs one real bad." The way that man looked, I could see why his wife needed a sense of humor. But I happen to think that everyone needs a sense of humor "real bad," no matter what his or her spouse happens to look like.

A sense of humor is not something you can order from the Sears-Roebuck catalog and give away. However, with a little help, all of us might be able to change our perspectives a bit and learn to see the lighter side of life.

If you're considering having a family, you might check with some people who've tried it successfully. All of them will tell you that if you don't have a sense of humor, it could be a very long life. Children want a parent who knows the difference between something that's funny and something that's deadly serious. Our youngest son wanted us to think his grades were funny, but it didn't work. Never once have we taken one look at his report card and dissolved in a fit of hysteria. We've had some fits, but we weren't laughing.

We did, however, think it was very funny when he wanted to take the family car to Florida for spring break when he was only fifteen. He told us it would be perfectly all right because he had this "older," more mature friend of sixteen who would do all the driving. We laughed for close to a week over that one. He, however, failed to see anything funny about it at all. You just can't depend on your children to let you know when something in the family is funny and when it isn't. Children are born trying to confuse the two.

Head 'Em Up . . . Move 'Em Out

I saw a family recently that looked as if they would have a great sense of humor. They'd thrown caution to the wind several times and had five children to prove it. You could tell they were very brave souls because they had ventured outside their home to eat in a restaurant. All five of those children were old enough that they were getting around on their own two legs—which means the parents' biggest task at that moment was to get all five children to go in the same direction at the same time.

That father looked like a cattle rancher whose herd was completely out of control. He was trying to round up tiny people who had no intention of going in the same direction at the same time. When he finally succeeded in getting them to the designated table, three of the children tried to jump into the same chair on top of each other. The one on the bottom was crying, the one on the top was kicking, and the one in the middle was screaming, "It's my chair. I was here first!"—totally ignoring the body under him. This is another example of middle-child syndrome.

I thought this was extremely funny. However, the parents failed to see the humor in their situation. (My husband said there was nothing unusual about children fighting over the same seat. Adults do it every day on the New York City subway.)

The father shot the mother a "look"; she flashed one back at him. I could read her mind. She was going straight home and have twin beds installed in the master bedroom with an electric fence around hers.

Anybody who thinks that children are born knowing the right thing to do never took one to a restaurant. A restaurant is a place where a child's imagination kicks in for the first time. They'll do things in front of total strangers they wouldn't dream of trying if they were eating at home.

When we left the restaurant, all five children were finally seated in their own chairs, and the parents were no longer speaking to each other. My hope is that somewhere down the road, maybe way down, this will be one of the funny stories they'll share with the grown-up children. It'll be titled "The Day Your Mother and I Decided Not to Have Any More Children."

A family provides the best place to learn to laugh. In almost any family there's at least one person who thinks you're funny, one who thinks you're not, and one who doesn't give a hoot. This provides great balance. On some days in your family you probably couldn't get enough popular votes to get elected to do the dishes, but it keeps life interesting.

In my own family, everybody thinks they're funny except Daddy. Momma is funny and she knows it. Daddy is funny and doesn't even suspect it. We were sitting around the den one night, and Daddy said, "I've been watching that 'Magnun P.R.' show." All of us laughed, but Daddy never knew why. For those of you who are just like my daddy, it's not the Magnun P.R. show; it's the "Magnum P.I." show. Subtle. But my family catches stuff like that—except for Daddy, that is.

In fact, a lot of the funny things that happen in our family seem to be about Daddy, because of Daddy, or about something that happens to Daddy. For instance, he's never been known as one who took much thought for external things, particularly his clothes. He just took the Bible literally on the "take *no* thought for what you shall put on" matter. Then he married Momma, and she took over the job of thinking about his clothes. Not only does she think about his clothes, she grieves about them.

He departed for a week's conference once and left his suitcase sitting on the front porch. It was no problem for Daddy. Momma washed his underwear and shirt every night, and he got along just fine. In fact, we're not sure he ever knew his suitcase was missing.

As long as he has everything covered that's supposed to be, he's as happy as a pig in clover. There've been times when my mother didn't think this quality of Daddy's was funny at all, but somehow over the years, she's learned to laugh about it.

We gained another "Daddy" story at my sister's wedding. She and Daddy were coming down the aisle. My sister had every hair in place and Daddy's hair has never figured out what place it's supposed to be. But it wasn't his hair. It was his bow tie. The thing had broken loose on one side and was hanging up and down instead of sitting left to right the way a bow tie should. That bow tie was flopping all over Daddy's chest, and all of us in the wedding party were so busy watching the bow tie come down the aisle, we forgot about my sister. When Daddy deposited her beside the groom and stepped in front of them to perform the rest of the ceremony (he's a minister), my sister spotted the bow tie and laughed out loud. Daddy never suspected a thing.

The best laughter comes from situations over which we have little or no control. It comes from the unexpected twists in life. Do you remember the theoretical question: If a tree falls in the forest and there's no one around, will there be noise? I think laughter is a bit like that. If something happens that's funny and no one has a sense of humor, is it still funny? Yes, it's still funny.

So if you haven't been catching the funny goings-on in your family, it's never too late to begin hearing, seeing, and picking up on them. This must have come naturally to my family. I grew up thinking I could draw a crowd simply by getting diaper rash. And when I drew applause by going away to college, I was addicted to it from then on.

Something Funny Goin' On, If You Can Just Figure Out What It Is

My daddy was always convinced that the rest of us never took anything seriously. My mother believed that anything serious deserved a good laugh. They were a great balance for each other. A perfect example of this was the time he and Momma were visiting my Aunt JuJu (I know it's a funny name; we'll talk about that later), and Daddy got up in the middle of the night to answer nature's call. My Aunt JuJu's house had a hallway with two doors located side by side. Daddy opened the wrong door and fell down the stairs into the basement. Momma heard all the commotion and flipped on the hall light just as Daddy began climbing back up the stairs on his hands and knees. She took one look and—to hear Daddy tell it— laughed hysterically for the rest of the night.

She says that this wouldn't have been funny at all if he'd been hurt. He says he was hurt. She says if he'd had anything broken he'd have never made it back up the stairs. He says, "What kind of a woman would laugh at a person who'd just fallen into the basement when all he wanted to do was go to the bathroom?"

Momma says he didn't just fall down the stairs; he skied down on his shins and never lost his balance once. Several things happened as a result of that trip to the basement. Daddy forgot all about where he had intended to go, and Momma gained another story to tell. It's difficult to figure out who enjoys the telling of this story the most—Momma or Daddy. And that's the way it's been for most of their lives together.

Family Trivia Gets Passed Down

The repetition of stories like this is an integral part of the lives of many families I know and love. There's a kind of family trivia game that exists in these families. When the family is gathered around the dinner table, someone will say, "Do you remember the time when Daddy fell down the basement stairs?" The story gets told, someone embellishes it a bit, and we laugh as though we've never heard it before. Someday one of the grandchildren in this family will be sitting around with his own children and say, "Did I ever tell you about the time Pappa Harney fell down the basement stairs?" The laughter gets handed down adult to child, mouth to mouth, heart to heart, warming yet another lifetime and bonding the future with the past. That's family trivia at its best.

There's always somebody in a family who will correct you if you tell a story without including all the details the way *he* remembers them. I've told the story of how my brother Jim was practicing gymnastics in the back seat of the car as we waited on Daddy outside a funeral home. Jim went flying out the car window and landed on the curb on his head. After hearing my version of that story, my brother called me to clarify a "few unimportant details."

He claims the entire incident was *my* fault. Says we got into a "discussion" over one of those wooden paddle toys with a rubber ball attached; that I won the "discussion"; and that in the last round of negotiations for possession of the toy, he went flying out the back seat window and landed on the curb. (We almost gave that funeral home its first chance to offer curb service, but fortunately, Jim didn't need it—just stitches.)

Now what would I do without my brother to remind me of all those delightful details that make me sound like Attila the Hun on wheels at a funeral home? You should see my brother's face—not from landing on the curb, but from the joy of telling this story. He lights up like the Christmas tree at the White House! And that's just part of the wonder of a family—remembering the stories, reliving them, and passing them on.

Some people decide early in life not to get along with their families. That completely baffles me. It's fairly close to not even liking yourself. Choosing not to get along with your family is like deciding you don't like your left leg and can get along without it. You'll find that you *can* get along without it—you can even go from place to place and learn to walk again—but your life will never be the same. Something will always be missing.

A family member is someone who is carrying around our own personal history in his head, and that should be extremely important to us.

The First Audition for Life

A family is the place where we try out for life. It's the place where we practice for life. We don't realize we're practicing, or we'd refuse to do it. But the family is the place where we try out our communication skills. We practice talking on our families. I think this is a great service. I didn't know how great it was until I paid 250 dollars to join a theatre class. The instructor was going to teach me how to talk. Well, for that kind of money I thought I should come out talking like Katharine Hepburn. Instead, I sounded just like I do today, and I had no money left.

That's when I developed a new appreciation for my family. They have put up with my talking all my life and have never sent me a bill. For as long as I can remember, when we're together, we practice talking. We are so good at it, we even talk for each other at the same time. My husband says my family is into doing phonetic aerobics.

Do you remember when you visited relatives as a child and you thought your aunts and uncles were the strangest people because they all talked at the same time, yet by some miracle they actually seemed to be able to keep up with what everybody else was saying? Now, when you catch yourself doing the same thing, you know this genetic quirk has finally caught up with you.

Everyone in my family learned to talk at an early age. When my brother Jim was only one and a half, he started mumbling one day and gesturing with his hands. I said, "Look, Daddy, he's trying to talk." Then I bent down to catch what he was saying, and he threw up on me. That may have been the last time I went out of my way to catch what someone else in my family was saying.

All this practicing within the family is just to perfect us for the outside world. If you wait to do your practice talking with total strangers, they won't appreciate it when you talk at the same time they do, or they may not be tolerant while you perfect the skill of getting your point across. This is known as "butting in," and my husband says I'm so good at it I could win an argument with my tongue tied to a tree. I know exactly where I learned it.

No one told me that a family is the place where you practice for life. This is a truth that may become clear to us only in retrospect. When as a child you became involved in a scuffle over some toy with one of your siblings, no one told you that you were learning the art of negotiation. When a difference of opinion interrupted family harmony and you reached an impasse—you know, the place where you either had to give in or leave home—you probably didn't realize you were learning the fine art of compromise. When my parents refused to budge an inch on their standards of what was right and wrong for themselves as well as their children, I learned from their example that values and principles did not fall into the negotiable category and that in certain areas there was to be *no* compromise.

We were allowed to argue our points when differences of opinion erupted, which they often did. But we knew beyond any shadow of a doubt that Daddy always believed he was right, whether we did or not. Somehow, though, we continued to practice having an opinion about everything from hem lengths to curfews. We were allowed to develop the confidence to speak our minds, to discover what our opinions were; then as long as we came around to Daddy's way of thinking, everything turned out fine. Momma always agreed with Daddy, and he agreed with her. That eliminated all that running back and forth between parents. There was no plea bargaining in our family. I know a lot of parents who could simplify their lives if they would agree to agree. A lot of children would grow up less confused.

Feel Free to Be Yourself, But You'd Better Have a Good Reason

The family is a place where you should feel free to be yourself. But, as is the case in the real world, you'd better have a good reason to back it up. One of our boys went through a stage when he was intrigued with making a gurgling sound in his throat. He seemed happy making this disgusting sound every waking hour. I finally said, "Son, why in the world are you doing that?"

He had a very nice reason. He said, "Because."

Now I've never met more than a few dozen parents who were weak enough to accept "because" as any kind of sensible reason for gurgling from sunup to sundown.

This happened to be the child who was into impersonations, so we had a bit of experience in listening to annoying noises. When "because" didn't float out the boat, he said he was practicing being a clogged drain pipe. I never did find out why he was practicing for it; there's never been much demand for clogged drains as far as I know. When we asked him to stop doing it immediately, he said, "Dad, you're always telling me to be myself."

"Well, son," my husband said, "that was before you decided you were a clogged drain, and if you persist in being clogged, we will be forced to have you unclogged. Do you understand?" I guess he did because that was the last time he felt free to be a clogged drain.

Some parent is always giving children brilliant pieces of advice—like to think for themselves, to use their imaginations, to be creative. The only thing wrong with brilliant pieces of advice is that usually the giver of that advice is never home when one of those creative minds kicks in and decides to think for itself.

I reached the point where I was almost afraid to be left home alone with all those creative minds. This kind of advice has always caused me undue stress.

Like the day I discovered that the elastic was missing from the waist of my favorite black skirt. I stomped up to the first hairy-legged person I could locate and yelled, "Okay, did you take the elastic out of my skirt?"

"Mom, use your 'inside' voice," the hairy one said. Sometimes my own words come back to haunt me.

"Stick to the subject, son. I'm standing here with a skirt that has a sixty-three-inch waist in it. What do you expect me to do, keep it and grow into it?" That was when he told me that he was just trying to be creative, to think for himself to solve a problem the way Daddy is always wanting him to do. So he used my elastic to try to patch a leak in his volleyball. Then the two of us had something in common. He had a useless volleyball, and I had a useless skirt that would fit an elephant.

Do you ever find yourself muttering under your breath, "When did I lose control?" I don't know whether this will make you feel any better, but you haven't lost control. You probably never had it to begin with.

The Place Where You May Give Out, But You Never Give Up

Very often it is years past an experience that you come to recognize it as a treasured part of your life. A close family friend of ours is an attorney who practices law so he can afford the luxury of calling himself a farmer. To hear his wife and children tell it, he grows a garden big enough to feed a small country. During growing season the children were required to hop out of bed at five-thirty in the morning—"the crack of dark"—and go straight to the garden. There they were to help pick beans, berries, or whatever happened to be "coming in" at the time. The father used this time for teaching lessons about God, for sharing the wonder of putting a seed in the ground and watching it grow, and in general for trying to pass on his love and respect for the land.

I don't have to tell you how much his children loved getting up at the crack of dark and dragging their little bodies outside. The daddy called this fellowship time—they called it torture. The youngest daughter once loudly announced to the good Lord and anyone else listening, "If I ever get out of this garden, I'll never get near another one as long as I live." That declaration came along several years before maturity set in. Now she plants her own little garden, takes her baby girl out, and sets her between rows so they can have "fellowship" while Momma picks beans.

So it may often be the tough times—the times we think there's nothing funny within six hundred miles of the place we call home—that make us stronger. They build our character whether we like it at the time or not. Times like these in my own family were probably the times I learned about discipline and thought work was definitely the only four-letter word my daddy knew. Those were the times when in the privacy of my room—just after I received something my dad thought was "for my own good"—I gnashed all my teeth and groaned, "Who dropped me into this mess?" As is the case in every family, those were the times when we children were convinced that our parents were put on this earth to make our lives miserable and that they were succeeding very well. But we didn't think that way for long. A bad attitude can set in if you're not careful, and when one does, it's a lot more difficult to get rid of than it was to acquire.

A bad attitude, when it's about your family, is a heavy coat to wear through life. Our family has had an occasional disagreement that raised the roof a few feet. We even practiced being mad with each other two or three times. We tried it, but nobody liked it because it didn't get any laughs. In fact, it didn't get us anywhere or anything but sad, and we weren't into that, so we practiced moving on to bigger and better things. Selective memory can be a great gift. That's when you choose the best and leave the rest.

These truths about our families will never change. You can write me a letter and thank me for telling you, or tell me you don't believe a word of it, but it will never change. A family is the place to practice for life and for whatever business you go into. It's where you should learn an appropriate response to nearly everything, and your family can be so appreciative. I had a performance just last week, and I gave the audience all I had. Three people applauded, and I thought, *Good grief, I got a better response than this from my family the day I put oatmeal and egg on my face to tighten my pores.*

We Didn't Laugh at the Time

My daddy has a few teeth that like to go out at night. Sometimes his teeth go out when they aren't invited. On one of our moves as a family, we were driving to our new town late on a Saturday evening. Daddy had to be there to preach his first sermon the next morning. Halfway there he asked if I would drive for a while. He pulled over, got out of the car, walked around the front, and got in on the passenger side. I had driven for about an hour when Daddy suddenly began to look for his teeth. But, his teeth were no longer with us.

He had placed them in his lap while he was driving and had forgotten about them. When he got out of the car to change places with me, his teeth took an unscheduled trip to the side of the road. We drove all the way back to look for them. None of us laughed at the time, especially not Momma. We found the teeth. They were no longer connected to

each other. We had most likely run over them ourselves as we pulled away.

Daddy has always known how to make a good
impression. He preached his first sermon in our new
church without his teeth, and the people liked him
anyway.

I guess everyone in my family just has some kind
of special talent. Momma can clear a room just by
taking her shoes off. And everyone has a story to top
everyone else's.

My husband is still learning all the rules of being
in a family like this. He's from a small, quiet family
and won't say much in front of a crowd, even when
he's related to them. He does great impersonations
but will only do his Foghorn T. Leghorn voice for me
if we're locked in the closet, the TV is turned off, he's
sure the telephone won't ring, and the dog doesn't
have her ear pressed against anything but her head.

We were riding along in the car once, and I
begged him to do his Yosemite Sam voice. I even of-
fered to pay him. He took my money but never de-
livered the goods. He claimed he was going to do it,
but about the time he opened his mouth, a car
passed us, and he changed his mind.

3

IF MY CAR COULD TALK, IT WOULD BEG FOR MERCY!
(The Family Car)

In the privacy of my own car, I conducted a new scientific study. This study concludes that the average American family spends two-thirds of its time in the family car. If you're wondering what in the world you do with the other third of your vast free time, you spend it finding a parking space for the car.

Everything traumatic that has ever happened to me has happened in the car. It happens either because of the car or because of what someone does in the car when there's no way to escape.

Every expert who owns a pen or pencil has written some kind of a guide telling us how to spend our leisure time. Most of their ideas have something to do with the car. They tell us to leave it all behind—to get away from it all. They tell us to revitalize our frazzled bodies and to get in the car to do it. You try giving this bit of advice to a mother of three children. This kind of advice is for children and dogs only. Children think anything to do with the car is "fun," and dogs will beg for a ride to the end of the drive just to pick up the paper. A mother of three children is a woman who doesn't have time to sleep, but if she did, she'd dream she was on her way to heaven and was having to carpool to get there. But chil-

47

dren—you show a fretful baby a picture of a car, and that baby will calm down instantly.

One time in my life I had fun in the car. I was so tired of listening to three kinds of music playing at once, the sound of video games being played, and the slam of tennis balls being thrown against the walls that I went out to the garage, got in the car, locked all the doors, and just sat there. That was fun!

You can get in your car to try leaving it all behind, then look behind to find it following you. You can try various methods, do it in various cities, and still fail to get away from most of "it." I did succeed in getting away from the house one year. The plumbing had backed up all the way to the windows, and we had no choice but to leave it all behind.

We thought we'd accidentally left one of the children behind in a wilderness store one summer. He beat us to the car, hid in the back, ate the food in the cooler, and spilled orange Kool-Aid into my suitcase. For the rest of that vacation I went around feeling like I had sand in my pants.

When a family travels by car, there's no getting away from anything. The family takes all of it with them and buys more of it from roadside stands along the way. This fact is made more complicated by the new mid-sized cars that will barely hold a family. My brother, his wife, and two boys came to see us last summer. They had everything from a baby bed, a beagle dog, a rubber raft, three fishing poles, six garbage bags of Pampers, and a magnolia tree strapped to the outside of the car. My sister-in-law was so embarrassed, she didn't want to come out of the car till after dark. She said, "We looked just like the Clampetts going down the road. People were afraid to pass us for fear something would get loose and hit them."

When you travel with children, you *have* to take everything they own just to keep them busy in the car. When children are in the car, they have the attention span of a bumblebee. Meanwhile, you are confined inside a vehicle with books that have most of the pages torn out of them. You spend so much time sitting on foreign objects that you think it's normal to be in pain. You have so many crackers smushed into the seat covering that you think they came with the car when you bought it.

You buy children's tapes to play in your wonderful automatic, built-in tape player. Then you have two grown-ups driving down the highway singing along with "Hippo in My Bathtub," with Dr. Seuss's entire library running around loose in the back seat.

This is part of the reason that years later as you are sitting around in an empty house you hear the sound of silence for the first time and think something is terribly wrong. You have to retrain yourself.

I Don't Know What It Is, but It's a Nice One

Traveling in the car gives you the urge to buy stuff you don't know what to do with or have a place for when you get home. I think it's the same phenomenon that makes college kids want to see how many people they can cram into a phone booth. Being away from home in the car forces you to buy items that are not even indigenous to the area you're visiting. We have a collection of sand dollars from Kansas City, Missouri, and some authentic Indian moccasins made in Taiwan and bought in Cleveland, Ohio.

My husband gave me a necklace made of Colorado gold, which he bought as a souvenir in Tupelo, Mississippi. He said it was the thought that counted. I came home from south Alabama with a large jeweled pin that says "Paris" on it. I didn't even know Paris was in Alabama. The boys bought sweat shirts that say "Ride the Big Wave" while we were in the Rocky Mountains. Does this make sense to you?

You can be out of town for three days and hunt down the nearest outlet mall where you will buy a cordless screwdriver for the same remarkably low price that you would pay at your discount store back home. What a deal! Once, when I was traveling with my mother, she begged me to stop at a roadside flea market. I had to send in a SWAT team to flush her out.

I bought a book on the history of the Grand Ole Opry from a bookstore in Little Rock, Arkansas. I'm from Nashville, Tennessee, for goodness sake. This syndrome is called the "I'm-out-of-town-with-my-family fever." The only cure is to go home and stay there.

If Getting There's Half the Fun—Drive Faster

You're a truly brave soul if you will venture past the city limits with a bunch of relatives in the car. It's just one of those things that seems like a good idea at the time. You start out on a trip and you say, "It's only three days, what could possibly go wrong?" Absolutely nothing—until you get a bunch of relatives confined within the four doors of anything on wheels.

I think this very experience must have inspired the story of the man who locked his family in the car and couldn't get them out for three days.

We took my in-laws out of town with us once.

My mother-in-law is one of the thoughtful types who thinks ahead. My father-in-law was the type who remembered when. So in three days time she did enough knitting to clothe half the state, and he talked us through the Great Depression six times. He had us stopping to pick up cans along the interstate, and she made us save our chewing gum wrappers. She said, "You just never know when something will come in handy." You'd have thought every rest area was a musical theme park with free admission.

It was such an interesting trip. Without it, I would never have known how many aluminum cans it takes to fill the extra space in my trunk.

I Turned Forty Inside My Car, And I've Had the Blues Ever Since

No one told you that after you have children you would never have a clean car again. But it's true.

Long before a male child gives up his pacifier, he'll want to sit behind the wheel of the car and practice driving and being sick at the same time. You can sit at home all day long with a child, and everything will be just fine. If that child is still in diapers, he'll wait till you get in the car to present you with a surprise that makes the dog want to leave home.

I used to wonder why the inside of my parents' car was so dirty. Then I got married and acquired my own family. I discovered that *I* had been one of the reasons my family's car was trashy. Children are uncomfortable riding in a clean car. They'll beg you to stop along the interstate to pick up items that have just been expelled from somebody else's car by a disgusted mother.

Children are born wanting to know how soon they'll be able to eat in the car, and sure enough, some of them eat on the way home from the hospital. There is some sort of unwritten belief that you haven't lived right until you've deposited a candied apple in the car.

When you go to trade in your car, the history of your family's eating habits—in fact your entire life together—is chronicled by the stains on the seats and carpet. You say, "Oh, look, that red spot is where little Leigh took up finger painting somewhere between Amarillo and Seattle when she was only three. And see that awful place on the floor where the carpet disintegrated. That's where little Brandt got sick after he ate the page out of Dr. Seuss's *Green Eggs and Ham.*

"And *that,*" you say, pointing to a window, "that window was cracked when the children were playing ice hockey in the back seat." That was the same day somebody lost his two front teeth. Actually, he didn't lose them; we knew where they were. Another child found them and fed them to the dog. That was a tough one for the tooth fairy.

The new cars today have voices that tell you everything you're doing and all the things you aren't doing, but they don't say anything about what you shouldn't do. The day somebody invents a self-cleaning car is the day I will have everything.

Food and Cars Are Unnatural Enemies

I have this recurring nightmare that I am trapped inside a car in a fast-food line.

My family knows that eating in the car makes my eyes bulge out. That's why we happened to find ourselves sitting in our car at a new Chinese take-out. Boxes were being passed out left and right, plastic forks were flying around, and I was getting dizzy. We were just getting into the aromas, passing the Chinese noodles, about to sip won ton soup from paper cups when it happened. All of a sudden those pieces of wood pulp impersonating dishes turned on us. Hollywood special effects technicians couldn't have planned it any better. Steven Spielberg may want to use us for his next disaster movie. Those dishes became acrobatic. I declare it was a regular Chinese circus. They went up in the air and landed upside down. When the car stopped reeling from five people grabbing at thin air and missing, we found ourselves with a five-course Chinese dinner on the floorboard.

There were several different interpretations of what went wrong. My husband says we were guilty of committing an unnatural act in the car. I'm inclined to agree.

I believe that eating in the car should be prohibited somewhere early in the marriage vows. But then I would have missed the pleasure of being stuck to the car seat by the biggest wad of bubble gum since the beginning of baseball and of walking into the bank one day with a Three Musketeers candy bar wrapper plastered to my behind.

The man who told me about it was so nice.

I have developed an unnatural fear of getting into my car after dark. It happened shortly after one of my nephews left a bullfrog in my car. The little thing died in there, and I came close. If my car could talk, all it would do is gag.

I turned forty sitting at a red light on the way to the dog pound to pick up a runaway dog—and I've had the blues ever since.

If There's a Silver Lining—This Is It!

It's true that a few unexpected mishaps happen in the car, but there's a surprise bonus that comes from being together in the car. This is very often the place where, uninterrupted by telephone or television, a family will open up and share with each other. Children not only love to eat in the car, many of them love to talk in the car. So be prepared to view travel time as a time to listen and share.

Some of our best heart-to-heart conversations have taken place in the close confines of those car doors. For some mysterious reason a child will surprise you by sharing something deeply personal. These become small moments with large payoffs— payoffs of growing closer, of growing in understanding of ourselves and our children.

So if you have to risk getting into your car once in a while, it's worth it!

4

THIS WAS
NO SURPRISE—IT WAS
AN AMBUSH
(The Family Vacation)

Noah, Mrs. Noah, all the little Noah's, along with two of every creature on the earth, spent forty days and forty nights afloat in a leaky ol' boat in a driving rainstorm. We don't have many details of the middle part of this trip and for that we should probably be grateful. In spite of the lack of day-to-day details, I can promise you this was not the dream vacation Mrs. Noah had always wanted.

We don't know anything about how they passed the time during their long journey, but I think Mrs. Noah spent it cleaning. We don't know how many times Mr. Noah said, "we're together, that's all that matters." We don't know how many times Mrs. Noah said, "Don't touch me, I want to be alone," and we don't know how many times the little Noah's said, "are we there yet?" "I'm hungry," and "where's the bathroom?"

While there are many things we don't know, I have always had a special place in my heart for Mrs. Noah. I think of her every year at vacation time.

A few years ago Chevy Chase starred in a movie called *Family Vacation*. It contained every disaster that could possibly happen to a family in a week of vacation. That picture was a smash hit. Families everywhere flocked to see it. I thought it was my life story. Until we saw that movie, I thought our family was solely responsible for proving that stupid law about how "everything that can go wrong will." We had one vacation where we proved laws that had been previously nonexistent like "what goes down will always come up."

Some people think that the reason a family should take a vacation is to rest. Don't believe that for a second. The only people who come home rested from a vacation are retired people. That's because they leave home with no children and they come back with no children. If you need rest, you better get it before you have children because you won't rest again for two or three decades. By then, you may be too tired to rest, but at least you'll have the time to try. My parents are just now beginning to rest after rearing the four of us. Every night, Momma rests on the sofa and Daddy does the same in his chair. Each accuses the other of sleeping and both of them deny it. They're just "resting" and while they have a good reason, they still feel guilty doing it.

A Brand New Discovery

My worst vacation trouble began when I opened my big mouth and told my husband that he never took us anywhere. That was my first mistake. I may have been pouting at the time, which was my second mistake. I even committed a third mistake by repeating myself just in case he wasn't listening when I ran it by the first time. After you've been married several years, you automatically assume that a husband isn't listening when you say something like that.

When I repeated myself and said, "I said, you never take us anywhere, anymore." He woke up and said, "Where's that?" (like he didn't know).

I said, "You know, *anywhere*, and I verbally underlined the word anywhere for emphasis which could have been my fourth mistake. I had momentarily forgotten that he had taken me to the auto value store to pick up new windshield wipers for my car and that even qualifies as going *somewhere* to a man.

I tried to drop the subject, but it was way past too late.

Then, my fifth mistake happened because of a magazine article. It was a magazine article which fell into the wrong hands—mine. My final error in judgment was to cut out the article and paste it over the steering wheel of my husband's car.

It was a simple article with simple suggestions for husbands, and I had a husband who occasionally needed a few simple suggestions. It all began with the headline. It read "Vacation on a Shoestring . . . Getaway to End All Getaways!" (That proved to be the only honest statement in the entire article).

I was guilty of feeling sorry for myself and of only reading the headlines. The one which said, "Delight your family with the unexpected and draw them together at the same time," sounded like something we needed. The article must have known what it was talking about because I wasn't expecting a thing when my husband called that morning in August. It was a brief conversation. All he said was, "Pack a *small* bag for each person (with special emphasis on the *small* part), be ready and waiting at the front door with the children, and be wearing a smile."

I don't think he grasped the full meaning of what he had just asked me to do. I could feel a bad mood movin' in. I didn't really care where we were going, I just wanted all my clothes to be going with me! A *small* bag won't even hold my makeup and if I had met him at the door wearing nothing but a smile, he wouldn't let me out of the house!

The boys were thrilled. Boys and women are total opposites in more ways than the obvious. Boys are always sitting on top of ready! All you have to say to get them excited are the words *go* and *surprise*. They rarely care where they're going; it's the surprise that counts.

Boys are especially happy if they don't have to pack any clothes. They want a bag full of computer games, toys, and things that shouldn't be permitted on airplanes. By the time we settled on what they could and couldn't take, I was distressed but under control.

I didn't know whether to pack sandals, a sweater, a bathing suit, or my hiking boots. Furthermore, I was going to be especially unhappy if I found I needed my hiking boots.

This was not one of the better mornings of my life. It was only the beginning of uncovering a new discovery about myself. I was beginning to suspect that I didn't like surprises! When the appointed hour arrived, we were all waiting by the front door—some of us were smiling—some of us were not.

The children were now less than happy because they couldn't take their friends with them. I tried to explain the situation, but frankly I didn't even understand it. I said, "Children, it's like this, we can't take anyone not related to us, because we don't know where we're going. When you take someone's child, and they can't bring any clothes, and you can't say where you're taking them, they're likely to have you arrested for having lost your mind, or for kidnapping—whichever they think of first."

"Why don't we know where we're going?" one child asked.

"Yeah," another said, "how can you go somewhere if you don't know where it is?" (This child had developed logic way beyond his years.)

Then, the third child said what he always says, "Whose big, fat idea was this, anyway?"

By the time the author of all this confusion rolled into the driveway, nobody was smiling. We did have our one small bag each, but nobody cared.

My husband was whistling and smiling simultaneously. This proves that it's much easier to smile when you *know* where you're going! He was having so much fun he couldn't figure out what was wrong with the rest of us, but he did notice we weren't smiling.

"Where's that big smile I asked you to wear?" he said to me.

"It wouldn't fit in my *small* bag," I answered.

He wasn't entirely without sensitivity because later he said, "Oh, honey, are you worried about not having enough clothes?"

"Now why would I worry about a little thing like that?"

"Don't worry, I'm sure you have everything you'll need. We're all together, and that's what counts," he assured me as we arrived at the airport.

We didn't have any bags to check because the ones we had were, you know, small. I fell asleep on the flight, and when I awoke, we were landing on an island the size of my bag! We landed on a runway so short the flight attendant said, "We are preparing to land," and "You may now unfasten your seat belts," all in the same breath.

We bounced down on the only island boasting of a runway the length of a pencil with an ocean view on one end, and an obstruction the size of a mountain on the other. There were fresh white wreaths hanging on the obstruction. One of the children said, "Look Dad, they hung flowers for us!" (He never knew how close to the truth that was.)

The airport was where the trip really began. It must have been used by the locals as a steam room. There were no towels, and there was plenty of waiting.

"Why do we need to wait in the airport, Dad?" said one of the sweaty children.

"Because we're waiting for the airplane to take us to the island where we're staying." Then, another child began to itch and proceeded to show us exactly where. . . .

When the plane arrived, I fought the overwhelming urge to ask for a crash helmet and a life jacket. The pilot came on the intercom and asked us to hold our breath during takeoff. I was way ahead of him. I didn't even look at my husband because to tell you the truth, at that very moment, I didn't like him much. "This is certainly one sure-fire way to draw the family together—forever," I muttered under my breath.

We took off. That plane spluttered, shimmied and rattled all over like a rock and roll band with no talent. Oil poured out of one engine in a steady stream. The children were thrilled—this was "fun"—but then children are born so parents can teach them how to have good sense, and it was obvious we weren't finished with these yet!

We made it into the sky, and then I realized that if we were headed for an island smaller than the one from which we had just taken off, it wouldn't be visible from the air.

No one told me we were in a plane that could land on water. So, when this plane took a nose dive and splashed down, I swallowed something I hadn't realized was in my mouth.

I was waiting to die when I realized that it shouldn't take that long. That was when I realized my fears about this island were true—it wasn't visible from the air. We were cruising around the ocean looking for it. When the pilot found the island and spluttered into port, I was just discovering how to breathe through my nose again.

Getting off that plane, I said, "I don't care if I have to learn to walk on water—I'm not getting on that again!" That was when I learned that we weren't on the right island, and we had to take a boat to get there.

That was my first time on the high seas, and I didn't realize my stomach could come up so far, so fast. Only one child had trouble. It was the same one who would be sick if he turned a corner too fast walking around the house. This child was so much fun to be around. I don't have to tell you what a good time we were having . . . but, we were all together.

That was how we got to the island. Once I was there, no one had to tell me why so many Americans relocate to the islands. They gladly give up family, houses, and friends to avoid the return trip home!

A Sense of Humor Will Help—
Twenty-five Years from Now

Even on a remote island, if you want to go somewhere, you rent something on four wheels to get you there. When our rental vehicle arrived on the scene and my husband said, "What's that?" I knew right away that we had no ordinary vehicle. The one thing I can say for it was that it was faithful. It stopped faithfully every two miles whether we wanted to or not.

I was in no mood to tour that island two miles at a time stuck to a bunch of sweaty people—but then no one had asked me what I wanted. I hadn't smiled since the steam room they called an airport. I only smiled then because I spotted another family who looked as if they were having almost as much "fun" as we were.

The fourth time that car made an unscheduled stop was right in front of a gas station. Actually, it was a shack with a broken-down gas pump out front. It had to be a "hot" spot; there was another car parked in back of it.

"Oh, boy, Cokes!" one child said.

"I'm still itching," said the second child.

"Civilization!" said another.

It's a mother's job to be optimistic, so I said, "It's a shack, is what it is."

They did have Cokes and directions to our "bungalow." (I could hardly wait to see that.) We went outside to get back in what by now my husband kept referring to as Hitler's final revenge. That's when we discovered that the keys were locked inside it.

You know, you can live with someone for a long time and never really know them till you see them in a real crisis. One of the boys even noticed something new—he said, "Look, Mom, Daddy has a funny vein that sticks out on his neck!" That was when I repeated what my husband had been saying to me ever since we left home. "It's okay, honey, we're together . . . that's all that matters." I don't think he believed me.

He looked up and said, "Well, what do you think would be cheaper, trying to get a locksmith down here from Nashville or breaking out the window and paying for it?" I never said a word. He already had the crowbar in his hands. It was so nice having that open window there. We especially enjoyed it every afternoon when it rained.

The Enemy Was Smaller Than a Shark And Just About as Deadly

There were moments on this trip when the enemy was "amongst us" as they say. We discovered we could turn on each other with no warning. My husband kept saying, "We're together—that's all that matters." By that time, I had a long list of other stuff that mattered, but he didn't want to hear it.

My husband was right about our not needing many clothes on this trip. There wasn't anywhere to go; there were hardly any people around, and the ones that were around weren't wearing very many clothes. My husband even noticed this fact and said, "Yeah, the brochure said, 'Vacation on a Shoestring,' not 'Wearing One.'"

We asked directions to a deserted beach where we could take the boys snorkeling. The children were out of the car and on the beach before we had the car in park. When we arrived, they were jumping up and down, beating themselves on the legs, and screaming.

"I've never seen them act like that," I said. About that time, I began jumping up and down, slapping myself on the legs, and screaming. Then my husband began jumping up and down, slapping himself on the legs, and screaming. I didn't know he could move that fast.

The enemy was not only smaller than a shark, it was invisible. Sand fleas by the billions were eating our bodies. We jumped, smacked, and yelped all the way to the water. No one had to tell us why that was a deserted beach.

I was running into the ocean fast enough to win something when the toe next to my big one struck an immovable object. I limped out to my husband with tears of joy in my eyes. By this time I was hoping he would notice how much fun I was having.

"What's the matter, darlin'?" he asked.

"It's nothing—just my toe."

"Here, let me look at it," he said.

"No! It's a very shy toe and won't come out of the water."

"Quit being funny," he insisted. "Let me see it!"

He inspected the toe while I looked the other way and cried.

"Did you have a toenail on this toe before we got here today?" he asked.

"I think so."

"Well, you don't have one now."

I wasn't a pretty sight. I was a long way from home. My toenail was gone. And I was *not* a happy person.

"What should I do?" I asked him. "Stay out here and bleed to death, maybe let a shark come and eat me, or go back on the beach so the sand fleas can enjoy me a ϙore at a time?"

About that time one of the children said, "Look, Dad!" and picked up a jellyfish. Then we had a mother with a toe the size of a cucumber and a child with a hand the size of a baseball glove. And—we were all together.

Sometimes Humor Is Nothing More Than Torture Recalled by a Feeble Mind

I've always wondered what it would be like for this trip to have happened to a family without a sense of humor.

The trip home was like a disaster movie in slow motion and reverse. All the children were in a bad mood because now that they *knew* where we were going, they didn't want to go.

The child with the big hand walked around as if we had tortured him into coming on this trip. He kept saying, "Don't touch me. I'm hurt!" My husband and I didn't have much to say to each other. My toe no longer fit inside any of my shoes. And a woman walked all the way across the airport just to step on it. I cried. Then one of the boys came over to comfort me and stepped on my toe again. I was still crying when we boarded the thing impersonating an airplane.

The pilot looked at me as if to say, "Why are you crying? We haven't crashed—yet."

Months later some friends of ours were getting married. They asked us for some honeymoon suggestions. To this day I don't know what came over us. We just couldn't help ourselves. We told them there was this delightful little island. . . . Those people are no longer speaking to us.

I learned a few things from that trip. I learned how to tell a tourist from a "local." The male tourist will be the one wearing a pair of black socks with wing-tipped shoes and Bermuda shorts. The female tourist will be the one with yellow hair and flowered Bermuda shorts with pantyhose under them.

And something else has happened as a result of that trip. It will be a very long time before I say, "You never take us anywhere anymore!"

It's Not Where You Go That Matters Most

When I was growing up, our family budget probably didn't allow for trips to an unknown island, and there were no theme parks. Mom and Dad would simply load us into the car and chug off down the road to a motel an hour away from home.

When Daddy pulled to a stop in the parking space directly in front of room 102, we'd come flying out of that car the way the bats come out of Carlsbad Caverns—in all directions at a zillion miles an hour.

We'd be in our swimming suits, and in the pool, before Daddy had the key out of the ignition.

Everybody swam, including Momma and Daddy. We must have gone to that place in the "off" times because there was never anyone else there. It was "our" pool. And now that I think about it, that motel probably never had an "on" time.

This pool was where we enjoyed the practice of chasing Momma, of begging her to go off the diving board backwards, of getting her wet when we knew she didn't want to be, of riding around in the water on Daddy's shoulders and jumping off at just the right place to splash Momma. We played let's-see-what-else-we-can-do-to-Momma games, and she still went back with us year after year. It wouldn't have been any fun without her.

This was the pool where I taught my baby sister to swim. She took to water like a tadpole, and by age two she was a pro. She was so tiny she can't remember learning to swim and can't remember going to this pool with the family. She just thinks she was born brilliant and with the ability to swim. I remember every single detail and frequently take credit for her brilliance. I especially remember the day I taught her to dive for the first time.

"Daddy, she wants to go off the diving board. Will you go up with her?" I yelled.

"*Who* does? . . . Miriam does?" he asked incredulously.

"Yes, sir, and you know how she is when she sets her mind on something."

"If you'll go up with her, I'll stay down here and catch her when she comes back up out of the water."

"She knows what to do. I've already told her," I added.

By this time, we had the entire family's attention. My brothers had gathered nearby treading water and watching to see what she was going to do next.

Momma was dog paddling out to the middle with one of her better looks of hysteria on her face. She yelled at Daddy, "James . . . now . . . she's too little to do that. . . . You just get off that ladder this minute. . . . What's gotten into you? . . . You're going to scare her to death! . . . Do you hear me? . . . She might never want to swim again."

Daddy said, "What kind of man do you think I am? . . . She *wants* to go up there. . . . I certainly wouldn't *make* the child do it! Good grief! I'm trying to hold her back!"

"Well, then, just let her go," Momma gave in. "She was born just like you, James Harney."

I'd been dog paddling all this time with my eyes on the little blonde thing climbing up the ladder with Daddy's arm around her. She had a grin you could drive a car through. She walked out to the end of that diving board like Evil Knevil. Daddy sat down behind her with his big hands securely around her little body.

"Otay, Sissie . . . I'm wreddy," she said. "Here I tome!" She was still discovering vowels and consonants but already learning to dive.

And while five Harneys held their breath, off she went. She went under just a couple of feet away from me. I already had my hands on her when she surfaced laughing and wearing the same silly grin.

She grew up to be a lifeguard during her college summers. Is it any wonder?

The six of us still reminisce about those trips to "the motel."

None of us remembers the name of the place, eating in the restaurant, or what the rooms looked like; but that pool sure brings back some memories.

Families today are blessed with the privilege of taking trips together that make my "pool" experiences pale by comparison. But family experiences are not valued by the amount of money spent making them nor by the distance traveled finding them. Family experiences are valued only by the mutual sharing; they are valued by the recalling and retelling year after year.

Different members of a family will have better memories of some events than others. My husband can barely bring himself to talk about the trip to the islands, but he loves to remind me that one of our worst experiences came about because *I* wanted to live in the country in an old house.

5

THERE'S NO SUCH THING AS A LITTLE ONE
(Family Mistakes)

There's an old saying that you should never invite trouble because it will accept the invitation every time. Well, we haven't had to send out invitations. Our troubles often come from something as innocent as having a dream. A dream is something you go into with your eyes halfway shut but will be forced to live through with them stuck wide open. Some of your dreams are best enjoyed in the dream stage, for when a dream begins to take shape in reality, it may be a nightmare in sheep's clothing. Our family had a dream like that. It started out in the shape of a country house.

Driving in the country one day we took a wrong turn and found our dream house. The house itself forced us to say words like, "Charming, isn't it? Doesn't it have *character?*" We took both our families out to see the house. It was the first time I can remember my family being speechless. My husband's dad said we might want to do something about the hole he could stick his arm through. We didn't see the hole because the house had charm. My best friend came out to see the house and she said, "My, how cute!" and "Isn't this sweet?"

Trust me—anything that is cute and sweet at the same time is either in diapers or will cost you more than you can make in a normal lifetime.

The house definitely had charm. The previous owner had charm. Even the realtor had charm. They ganged up on us and charmed us into ignoring the fact that this house was 125 years old. It was so old it was nothing but a skeleton covered with paint. They charmed us into ignoring the fact that the kitchen, family room, and upstairs rooms had no heat. They told us of a principle we'd never heard before—that heat rises. They failed to tell us that before heat can rise it must have a point of origin.

There was practically no end to the charm we encountered. The two-acre yard was just full of it, particularly since we didn't own a lawn mower. There's just no way for you to know how much my husband enjoyed standing waist deep in grass trying to hack his way back to the house.

You know the old saying "Charm is deceptive, and beauty is only skin deep"? I always thought it was coined by a husband who married a lady who wore too much makeup, but *no!* It was coined by someone who was forced to live in a house like this one.

This place had more charm than a vacuum cleaner salesman or the Avon lady. And I know it had character because that's what you say about people who are off their rockers and houses that have lived way past their prime. Somehow, when we signed the papers, we managed to gaze right past reality straight down the yellow brick road, which may have something to do with the color of the house— yellow—the color of daffodils. I will always associate daffodils with people who are off their rockers.

We packed up our little family and moved to the country with a line from one of John Denver's tunes running through our minds: "Move to the country . . . blow up the TV . . . teach the kids about Jesus." It sounded so wonderful. . . . It was nuts is what it was!

All You Need Is Another Mouth to Feed

A dearly devoted family friend wanted us to experience all the joys of being in the country. He gifted us with a cow that had been a rodeo star in her previous life. Her favorite activity was kicking up her heels, preferably in someone's face. The first week we owned our cow, she was forced to live in the dog pen.

I told my husband that we needed to "plant" a fence. He told me that you do not "plant" a fence. But I don't see why not; they go in the ground like everything else. You can see I was prepared for country life.

Our cow was a bit crowded in the dog pen, so one day we moved the doghouse out of the pen to give her more space until we could "stake" a fence. When the doghouse was lifted out of its resting place, millions of killer bumblebees took flight. They weren't angry. They were mad! They lit on the first thing in sight that happened to have four hooves. That cow looked like she was practicing for her next rodeo. She was a cow gone totally insane. (I wasn't far behind her.) Her head and tail were saying hello to each other about every two seconds. I'm pretty sure she attempted a triple somersault and landed on one hoof.

I was proud of my husband—he'd be great in the middle of an attack from outer space.

"Grab the hose pipe," he ordered. "Get the kerosene! Find me the matches—now!"

I was afraid he was about to set the cow on fire.

"Here's the hose pipe, Dad," our son said.

"Son! . . ."

The boy was just standing there with the hose in his hand, waiting. "What?"

"Do you think I'm going to beat them to death with the hose? Turn it on! Point it toward the cow and leave it on her!"

He grabbed the kerosene; dumped it in the nest; yelled, "Stand back"; threw a match into the nest; and ran to safety.

The last time we saw those bumblebees, they were headed for the coast of Florida. My one regret is that we didn't go with them.

All That Shivers Is Just Plain Cold

That August some of our friends gave us a housewarming. They gave it during the wrong month. We needed warming in December, January, February, and March. Winter came—and winter that year was the coldest since the "war."

I kept saying, "Are we having fun yet?" If we were I didn't want to miss out on it. My husband perfected glowering and scowling. Our youngest son thought it was his job to inform us that it was too cold, and our friends stopped coming to see us.

Trying to bathe in the 125-year-old bathroom made chills run up and down our spines, except that it was so cold the chills didn't go anywhere—they hung around. The claw-foot bathtub took three hundred gallons of water to fill. We were on well water, and I learned the real meaning of the "trickle down factor." The water pressure was so bad that if I turned on a hair dryer, the water went off.

The day my husband said, "Cheer up, things could be worse," I wanted to clobber him.

You Don't Even Have to Cheer Up—Things Will Get Worse Anyway

One morning we were in the bathroom together. We had to stick together in case either one of us got hypothermia.

But, listen, when you're freezing and you're already miserable, don't waste time getting hypothermia—get hysterical. That at least creates body heat.

"Look at this!" I exclaimed.

"What?"

"My hair! It's moving!"

"What's so incredible about that?"

"Listen to me! My hair is *moving*—it's blowing. There's a breeze blowing through the wallpaper. I'm going home to my mother. Not even my mother would want me to live in a house like this. She told me once that when you'd made your bed, somebody could make you lie in it, but they couldn't make you change the sheets. I think this was what she was talking about." I was babbling like a maniac when he finally looked at my hair.

"Yes, I see your hair blowing," he said. He knew I didn't really want to go back to my mother, but you can get desperate when there's a gale wind blowing through your bathroom wall.

"And I can see your breath too," he continued. "Come spring," he said. And I knew what he meant.

"We can't just . . . up and move . . . again . . . can we?"

"Watch us!"

January precedes spring in our part of the country. It preceded it by about three years that winter. New Year's Eve the temperature reached a record low, and so did we. All the pipes in that house exploded.

We lived with friends for three weeks while my husband became a plumber. I went out every few hours with hot coffee. The poor man had icicles on his beard and arson on his mind. He kept saying, "When spring comes . . ."

"Yes, darlin', I know." I don't think he liked being a plumber.

Then he'd crawl back under the house muttering something about having a long talk with John Denver about *that* song.

When spring came, I was already packed. Then the rain began. That's when we found out that the "ditch" behind our house was a raging river. People we've never seen before floated down our ditch on life rafts. The neighbor's barn disappeared, and Suzy, the cow, learned to swim.

When the waters receded, we backed the moving van up to the house. The last piece of furniture was just being put on the truck when the mold set in.

I've never seen a moving van leave rubber before. We left a cloud of dust on all that charm—and I think we cleared a new road on the way out.

If you're lucky, you can learn from your mistakes. If you're lucky and smart, you never make the same mistakes twice. I learned a lot from this mistake. I learned that being in the country did not necessarily make a family grow closer. Growing closer is something that can happen in a small uptown apartment just as well. I learned that my husband enjoys old houses about as much as he enjoys a root canal. And I learned that I could come dangerously close to losing both my mind and my sense of humor, but that my appetite was as big as ever.

I learned that when you've made a mistake and you know it, you always try to blame the people you love most. My husband looked at me on several occasions and said, "This would have never happened if you hadn't wanted to live in an 'old' house." I told him it was his fault because he agreed to go along with me and because he liked that John Denver song. You always think you'll feel better if you can find somebody to blame, but it never works.

Oh, there were other things we learned. My husband didn't know that the kitchen had anything to do with romance until we lived in that house. He learned that romance takes a sharp nose dive when the still temperature in the kitchen is thirty-five degrees on a "good" day. He learned that cows eat too much and that grass grows too fast.

If There's a Mess to Make, The Family Wants in on It

The only way I can think of to avoid some serious mistakes after you're married is to give serious thought to them before you get married. You may think you know a person, but until you've seen that person with a roll of wallpaper or a paintbrush in hand, you don't know the person at all.

Every engaged couple should be required to wallpaper, paint, and practice moving furniture before they get married. That is the quickest way I know to find out just exactly what you're getting yourself into.

The person who said, "Love conquers all," had never been left in a nine-by-twelve room with the object of his affection and a can of wallpaper paste. Wallpapering can turn the most even-tempered man into a raging lunatic. You can take a man who seems to have almost no personality, put a roll of wallpaper in his hand, and his true personality will bubble up to the surface in no time. He'll become fluent in languages you didn't know he could speak.

Have mercy on the woman who succeeds in coercing a man to help her wallpaper. He'll want to do all the measuring and cutting . . . just so it will be done right, you understand. Then, when he cuts it too short, he'll blame you for it while he's standing there with the Exacto knife still in his hand.

It's possible that wallpapering could even be used to clean up the criminal justice system and empty our prisons. If you put a newly arrested felon in a room with nothing to do but wallpaper, you'd have a confession within thirty minutes.

If prisoners had to wallpaper every day while serving out a sentence, they'd be rehabilitated so fast your head would spin.

They'd be begging you to let them go clean for the rest of their lives—anything but spend their remaining days cutting, pasting, and smoothing out bubbles.

My husband says, "What kind of a sentence is it that lets a man watch television, exercise, read, and go to school?" You make it public knowledge that prison is nothing but one great, gigantic, endless room to be wallpapered for all eternity and the crime rate would plummet overnight. You'd have drug dealers begging you to let them manage Meals on Wheels in no time.

It's the same when it comes to painting together as a family. But in my case I like to paint even less than my husband likes to wallpaper.

How Many Relatives Does It Take to Paint a House?

I don't like to paint—never did. I didn't like finger painting as a child. It's a stupid idea to put paint all over yourself and smudge it onto a piece of paper. Then what do you have when you get finished? You have a piece of paper that looks as if somebody wiped his hands all over it, a "work of art" that only a mother would hang up. And you have paint squashed up under your fingernails in places that soap won't reach. That's why I never liked finger painting, and I wouldn't be crazy about doing it with any other part of my body.

The aesthetic value of painting improved for me only slightly with the introduction of brushes. That was when I learned that I didn't like painting trees on paper, not even with a brush. Then we progressed to drawing and painting tiny little houses on paper with our tiny little brushes. I found I did not like painting tiny little houses with my tiny little brushes. So it's no great surprise to learn that I enjoy painting even less now that I'm an adult and the brushes are even larger.

We bought a house after dark once. We had just run away from the 125-year-old pile of sticks that tried to kill us. We bought the first house we found that had heat in every room, floors, and bathrooms that actually did what they were supposed to do.

When we went out to look at the house in the light of day, my husband said, "Well, that settles it. This house needs a good paint job."

I said, "This house doesn't just need painting. It's down on its hands and knees begging for it—and I hate painting."

"Give me those papers," I said to the real estate agent.

"Why?" my husband said.

"Because I'm going out on the porch to set fire to them. I'm not painting this house." Now you can see how much I love to paint. You can also see how I came to own a house that needed painting.

When you have a house that needs painting, you learn that putting the stuff on the walls is a lot easier than getting all the colors to match. I learned that painting makes my nose quit working, makes my head ache, and makes my mother and daddy drop in—to "help."

It isn't normal for a family to paint together. Mental hospitals are full of entire families who have tried painting together. I am telling you that once a family has walked to the edge of reason holding paintbrushes in their hands, there is no going back. It doesn't matter what kind of brush it is. You can purchase the finest brushes money can buy, the ones with bristles snatched from the tail of some unsuspecting animal. You can have brushes with individually customized handles made of wood from the Holy Land. If the brush is hanging from a hand belonging to someone to whom you're related, the only thing he'll be able to cover with one coat is himself, the floor, or anything else you do not want painted.

You can go so far as hiring a professional painter to give lessons in stroking techniques. But you may as well put your money in the commode and flush it!

My daddy wanted to paint the sun porch, so I felt it would be nice to give him a little advice. Have you ever tried giving your father a little advice? Fathers don't take advice; they're immune to it since they only have experience in giving it.

I said, "Daddy, you need some help with your strokes."

He said, "I've never had a stroke in my life; I'm the picture of health."

"No, Daddy, I'm talking about your stroking technique."

"Why? Are we going swimming?"

See what I mean? He was slopping paint on the wall in every direction, and he'd never heard of stroking technique. That's why the room he painted looked as if it had been hand rubbed with a wet tennis shoe.

My sister was even getting in on some of the "joy" of painting our house. And the son who claimed back trouble when it was time to mow the yard was begging to be a part of all the fun. We held out on him as long as we could because he had been in a "little" trouble at school over painting. During recess he finger painted a wall that the school hadn't wanted painted. Then we were forced to make a donation so the wall could be restored to its original color. After all that trouble they didn't even name the wall after us. And that same child was now promising us he'd do anything we wanted—he'd even go to college—if we'd just let him paint.

Being the tough parents we are, we gave in. We selected a place where we thought he'd be capable of less damage—the laundry room. It was small, but I soon learned that there has never been a room small enough to be turned over safely to a twelve-year-old boy with a gallon of paint.

When we gave him his own gallon of paint, you'd have thought we had plopped a Harley-Davidson in front of him. He was ready to go. I left the scene right away.

Don't you agree that all mothers have an extra sense when something awful is about to happen? Well, I do—and I did. But my husband told me this would be a good experience for the boy.

Meanwhile, in the rest of the house, my momma and I were painting in the bedroom, my husband was painting in the entrance, Daddy was whistling a tune while destroying the sun porch, and my sister was attacking the living room like an escapee from art school. Every now and then, just to assure myself that I was still alive, I staggered out to the entrance to stare at my husband.

He said, "What's wrong, honey? Your face looks like it's been stretched over a volleyball."

I may have looked like a volleyball, but I felt like Jack Nicholson in *One Flew over the Cuckoo's Nest*.

Sometime in the middle of all this confusion I remembered that we had turned the laundry room over to a minor. If there's anything that comes even close to what a woman feels like in the middle of childbirth, this was it. She doesn't want to stick around for the finish—she just wants to know which way is out.

We came around the corner and stood in the doorway to what looked like a paint-testing ground. This was where we proved once and for all that we were good, loving parents. We decided to let him live.

"What is *paint* doing in my best Tupperware bowl?" I yelled.

"Well, I needed something lightweight I could carry around with me," he began.

"You've been carrying around a brain for years," the boy's father said.

"And I want to know *why* there are white tennis shoe prints all over the kitchen floor?" I yelled.

"Mom, *that* happened after I turned over the gallon of paint, and I went into the kitchen for the Tupperware bowl and some paper towels to clean up the paint. When that didn't work, I just decided to use the paint off the floor to paint the windows, and then I thought maybe you might not want the windows painted . . . so I went back into the kitchen for another rag. Then that's when I dropped the Tupperware bowl on my legs, and . . ."

"Stop!—Hold it right there!" my husband broke into this fascinating monologue. "Son, listen to me . . . we still love you, but, son, you have hereby had your license to use paint revoked—whether you ever go to college or not!"

That boy had so much paint on him we carried on this entire conversation not realizing we were talking to the back of his head.

Well, we finished the painting, and we're still speaking to each other. But you need to know what you have when you finish painting a house with your family. You have a house that looks as if it's been stuccoed from the inside out. And you also need to know how many relatives it takes to paint a house in case you ever lose your mind and decide to try it. It takes only five to paint it, but it takes fifteen to clean up the mess.

After the experience of painting this house together, my family thought we'd shared everything there was to share in life.

We forgot about things like the flu and other invisible viruses.

6

ANYBODY CAN BE
SICK—IT TAKES TALENT
TO BE PITIFUL
(In Sickness and Health)

There was a period of time while I was growing up when I wanted to be a nurse. Then came the day one of my little brothers fell and broke his arm. I took one look at him, saw his elbow facing in the wrong direction, ran into my bedroom, and hid in my closet for hours. I didn't feel well for a long time after that. That was only the first of many incidents that would teach me something about myself: Sick people make me sick!

I know you're relieved that I'm not a nurse, but you couldn't be *half* as relieved as I am. I left the doctoring up to my brother, Rodney, and the nursing profession in the probing hands of my sister, Miriam. Now I go around trying to make people better by making them laugh. Great teamwork, don't you think?

When I go to see my brother, I make him take off his white jacket and stethoscope. I can walk into his office feeling perfectly well, but seeing that white coat and the metal thing hanging around his neck . . . I get sick every time.

When my husband and I were getting married and were reciting our vows and the pastor said, "in sickness and health," I felt weak in the knees. That was not the place I should have felt weak in the knees. It should have been the "for richer, for poorer" part. I just didn't know it at the time.

There's a definite pattern to our sickness and health. My husband gets sick and passes everything on to me. I've never been one to get depressed during Christmas. And now that I've been married to someone who gets sick at Christmas, I'm usually too sick to be depressed. What's a little flu at Christmas? Who cares if you walk around with a box of Kleenex strapped under your nose? Who cares if your legs feel like warmed-over Jell-O? Your family won't care. People out shopping won't care. Why, you probably see people out shopping who look worse than that—and they don't have any excuse!

I don't see any reason to be depressed just because everyone else has a home scented with Christmas tree potpourri and mine smells like Vicks salve. For years my husband thought Vicks was my own special designer fragrance during the month of December.

I was brought up to believe that Vicks salve was the cure for everything. We were probably the only family whose children carried Vicks salve to school every day in their Mickey Mouse lunch boxes. One day somebody stole my Vicks out of my lunch box, and I was afraid I'd get sick before I could get home and tell Momma so she could replace it. When I told her about its being stolen, she wasn't even upset. She said, "That's all right. The poor child must have been coming down with something."

Yep—most likely a weird case of stealing things that smell bad.

The first Christmas that my husband and I came down with a cold at the same time, he pulled out a jar of Mentholatum at bedtime; I grabbed my Vicks salve. We went to bed with Vicks rubbed all over our chests and globs of Mentholatum under our noses. We smelled so good we couldn't get near each other for fear of being overcome by the fumes.

Years later I found out that Vicks doesn't cure anything; it just smells so awful you forget about how bad you feel. My momma still believes that the reason I stay so healthy is that she exposed me to Vicks at such an early age.

Every woman has good motivation for not getting sick. My mother was never sick when I was growing up. She was motivated by the fear that Daddy would get loose in the kitchen.

If It Can't Be Seen With the Naked Eye, You Don't Want It

I've always been curious about those people who were the very first to coin new sayings, like "I'd have to get better just to die" and "I'd have to reach up just to touch bottom." Until someone comes along to inform me otherwise, I am going to believe that they were the first mortals in history to catch the flu while visiting relatives at Christmas.

My family waited until we were all grown before we tried being sick together. We waited until spouses and innocent children were involved. There was one year when you could tell it was Christmas by the cars lined up on the driveway. You could tell by the packages stacked up under the tree. But you could *not* tell by the people lined up down the hallway.

It was two bathrooms, ten adults, five children— and plenty of waiting. You can spend most of your earthly life with your family. But when the flu virus is involved, they won't even come close to looking familiar. You can spend years being on good terms with those people. But when it comes down to the basics of being sick together, prisoner-of-war training camp couldn't prepare you for what you encounter.

Your mild-mannered father, who would give you the food off his plate and pretend he'd already eaten, will have a personality change that makes Superman look like a fraud. When my daddy saw the line outside both bathrooms, he missed a beautiful chance to become the first cat burglar in the history of our family. I do believe he would have scaled a two-story wall with his bare hands to break into one of those bathrooms trying to spell relief.

When your entire family is sick at the same time, you learn quickly not to put much faith in the old rule of "women and children first" or "first come, first served." It's every man, woman, and child for themselves. A sixty-year-old grandmother with a virus will trample Santa Claus to get to the bathroom first. And you may as well know this: Those spouses who had you convinced they would die for you—believe me, they won't.

People do things they won't even recall later. My husband doesn't even remember being sick that year. Selective memory loss can be an advantage at certain times in life, and this is one of those times.

We got to know each other extremely well that Christmas, and the best part of it was that most of us chose to forget about it. Except for me, and as you can see, I rarely forget anything.

If You Bring It Home—You Have to Share It

I was brought up in a "close" family. We were taught that a family should share everything—the hurts, the joys. We learned to cheer when someone captured a title, brought home an *A*, or grew another inch on the wall. In a few cases we even cheered a *C*. We always sang at birthdays and applauded when baby teeth fell out. Some of mine stayed out so long we applauded when the replacements finally showed up. We anticipated everything from the tooth fairy to the annual showing of *The Wizard of Oz* (after we got our first television set). We always missed *The Wizard of Oz* because it was always shown on Sunday night when we were at church. But that didn't stop us from anticipating it. I was twenty-three before I saw *The Wizard of Oz*, so I anticipated it for a long time.

Those were "normal" occasions to applaud— times of laughter and sharing. The longest summer of my life was the one when we shared the mumps. No one was even anticipating them, but they showed up anyway. With the near extinction of this childhood illness, families are now missing this rare opportunity for sharing . . . and they should be down on their knees every day being thankful. Childhood illnesses used to have a language all their own, similar to the computer jargon of today. For instance, you didn't just catch something, you "came down" with it. That's picturesque.

The summer we came down with the mumps was in many ways historic in my childhood family. I was the first little person who came down. My body gave the mumps a trial run to see how I liked it. First, one side of my neck and face puffed up like a balloon for two weeks. Then I returned to school for three days, at which time my body decided to bring the mumps back for a command performance lasting another two weeks. It was so nice.

My brothers were so good to me. They laughed, slapped their sides, and poked sour pickles in my face while I was sleeping, which made my eyes water and my overblown cheeks constrict.

I missed close to a month of school that spring. Let me put it another way. I didn't exactly "miss" it. I just wasn't able to attend. And as happens in every family, he who laughs first doesn't necessarily laugh last. My brothers got close to me, and while they were laughing in my face, I breathed in theirs.

Two weeks later their cheeks started to pucker. They started to bloom. They puffed and bloomed so long we almost had to move to a bigger house to hold their cheeks. You could have packed enough luggage in them for a weekend trip—with room left over for a picnic lunch.

Those boys' cheeks were so big that one afternoon when Daddy came home he said to Momma, "What are those sacks of potatoes doing on the living room sofa?"

"What potatoes?" she asked.

"Those!" he said pointing.

"Those," she said, "are cheeks! And if you look closely, somewhere under those cheeks are your two sons."

Momma was worried. She said, "Just how much do you think their cheeks can take?"

I wasn't worried. I was too busy being satisfied. I treated those boys like a side show. I said, "Daddy, get out the movie camera."

"Why, Sis?"

"'Cause, Daddy, when they grow up, if they get too big for their britches, we can show them movies of when their cheeks wouldn't even fit into their britches."

Daddy liked that idea. He broke out the camera and captured on film what had to be the two biggest cases of mumps in history. And that was the first time in Daddy's movie-making career that he didn't cut off the heads of his subjects.

Once we showed this film to some family friends. We decided not to tell them that Jim and Rodney had the mumps and see what reaction we'd get. The film was clicking away. Suddenly, there they were—two boys grinning from ear to ear. You could no longer see their ears, but I'm sure they still had them. Those boys looked so proud—you'd have thought they had been selected to star in a Crest commercial.

There was a moment's silence before one of the friends spoke up.

"Excuse me," the wife said, "but what in the world are they carrying on their shoulders? Footballs?"

I don't have to tell you how many times we watched those movies. Anyone who needed a good laugh would say, "Let's get out the mumps movies." And all these years later, I can get anything I want from my brothers. I just mention the mumps movies, and those guys will follow me anywhere.

Pitiful Pearl

There's rarely anyone as sick as the man, woman, or child who decides to be pitiful. Being pitiful is a popular condition. Why, doctors' offices would probably be half empty if it weren't for the "Oh, Poor, Pitiful Me" complex.

I have a little experience with this condition myself—just enough experience to know that being pitiful doesn't work unless someone notices and verifies that you are truly, truly pitiful. There's just no satisfaction in working up a good case of pitiful unless someone is around to appreciate it with you.

I don't think our family invented the "Oh, Poor, Pitiful Me" complex, but I may be the first person to isolate the illness and give it a name. Now my family is doing all it can to keep it from dying out.

It's funny. When you work up a real pitiful attack, your husband or wife will always try to make you smile. They don't want you to smile so you'll feel better; they want you to smile so *they'll* feel better. There's nothing worse than standing around feeling pitiful with someone trying to force you to smile.

If you felt like smiling, you wouldn't be pitiful in the first place. Once when I was practicing the art of being pitiful, my husband walked up behind me and said, "Excuse me, have we met before?"

Isn't that cute?

"As a matter of fact, you have not met me before," I said. "I am no longer the person you used to know. I have allergies, in case you haven't noticed." I sniffed a little too. Sniffing always makes you seem more pitiful. "The person you knew didn't have nerves that were shattered and arches that had fallen. She could talk without her voice quivering and drink from a glass without help," I said before I sniffed again.

"Excuse me," he repeated. "Is that what I get for trying to put a smile on your face?"

"If you wanted to be with someone who smiled all the time, you should have married a beauty queen—that's what they do best. When I'm ready to smile again, I'll let you know," I said feebly. "I'm suffering from a terminal case of allergies. My feet keep going in different directions, and total strangers stop me on the street to ask if I need help. I'm pitiful, just pitiful, and nobody cares. Why, I'm so pitiful that today I walked into the paint store and asked if they had a size seven-and-a-half medium in something black.

"I'm tired," I said, walking into the bathroom. "And I'm going to get in the shower and stay there."

He shook his head. I knew exactly what he was thinking. He was thinking a good hot shower would clear up everything.

Well, the last thing that was perfectly clear to me was the directions on Kaopectate when I was in Mexico.

So I have a little advice for you. If you feel like being a little pitiful, you'd better have some reason other than allergies. You could get a broken leg and your family would rally around you. They'd become instant gourmet cooks and then leave the kitchen looking like Egypt after a swarm of locusts. But an allergy must be borne in abject misery and desolation—no cooking, no cards, and not much sympathy.

Sometimes when you least expect it, you will get a little sympathy as long as there is something "real" wrong with you.

Once when I was trying to exercise my body into submission, I sprained a knee and was forced to give it a rest for a few days. I got the sweetest handmade card from one of the boys. It said, "I was going to buy you some knee socks, but I didn't know what size your knees are." I felt better immediately.

This was the child who made a lovely bouquet of ragweed and daffodils and put it by my bed during one of my worst allergy attacks. I know it's the thought that counts, but it made me feel so sorry for my daddy.

When he was walking around with his head in a cloud of ragweed, we called him Phineas T. Fogbound. When his eyes resembled matching slots on a video game, we made your-eyes-look-like-road-maps-to-China jokes. We subjected him to physical humiliation. We took advantage of his weakest moments—those times he was too bleary, sniffly, and sneezy to defend himself. He was a walking TV commercial, and we did things to him we wouldn't have done to our ninth-grade math teacher.

We cut up cucumber slices and plastered them on his eyes. "They'll relieve the burning," we assured him.

We took frozen tea bags and taped them over his face. We laughed in the face of his runny nose and quivering lips. And, if that weren't enough, we took pictures.

Now we show those pictures to the grandchildren. It's, "See Papa Harney when he wore cucumbers. . . . See Papa Harney when he was impersonating a teapot. . . ."

In a family like mine you learn early to suffer in silence. Very often the attention you get can be worse than the ailment.

If something on my body hurt, I learned not to tell anyone related to me by birth. Rodney always wanted to put his ear to it. (He became a doctor.) Jim always wanted to tap on it with a tool. (He's a supervisor of quality control in an automotive plant.) My sister would poke it hard and say, "Does this hurt?" (She's a charge nurse in critical care.)

So if you value your health, you keep it to yourself in a good-sized family. Except when it comes to being pitiful, someone in your family needs to know, because he or she just might be the cure you need.

I was visiting my brother one day when his youngest little boy came in the house sounding terribly pitiful. His bottom lip was stuck out so far we could have set lunch on it. Leaning down with open arms, his mother said, "What's the matter, darlin'?"

He sort of whimpered, he sniffed, and his lip wobbled all over the room. He mumbled something totally unintelligible as he fell into her arms. Then I caught the words, "Momma, me want you." He repeated it, "Momma, me want you." It hurt my heart. But it was nothing more than a very important case of Pitiful Pearl coming to visit. All he needed were Mommy's arms, a comforting voice, a little encouragement, and suddenly Pitiful Pearl was nowhere in sight. A child's need to be cuddled and comforted should only be exceeded by a loving parent's ability to cuddle and provide comfort.

One of our boys came in one afternoon and told me he had a bad cut on his finger. I said, "Let me look at it. Where is it?"

"There . . . right there, by my fingernail." Then he looked at me as if to say, "How could you take so long to see this mortal wound?"

"Get me my magnifier," I said. "Is this it?"

"That's it! Don't touch it! It's bad, real bad!"

"Son, it isn't a cut; it's only a hangnail," I said.

"Well, it needs a bandage on it!"

It took me a while as a mother to realize that when this happened what he really needed was some extra love, some tender sympathy, and that his need had nothing whatsoever to do with the hangnail. Emotional needs go much deeper. I learned that very often we don't really know how to verbalize our deepest needs; we just want those who love us to be there for us. I also learned that sometimes a Band-Aid carefully applied where it is not even needed spells love to a child. We had a child like that.

It doesn't take much for a mother to work up a visit from Pitiful Pearl. You listen to so many tales of woe, you feel like a walking 911 number. Finally you hear one tale too many and decide that your day has come, that you need attention just like the rest of the family.

The day this happened to me, I took my pitiful self into my bedroom and locked the door. When my family found me, they tapped on the door.

"Honey, are you in there?"

"No, I'm not here right now," I said, "but you can leave your name and number and any brief message you wish." I stressed the "brief" part.

"Honey, quit kidding around," he said.

"I'm not kidding around. I said a brief message, and I meant it."

There was this long pause; then he said, "Okay, a brief message . . . 'They don't say Hanes until we say they say Hanes!'"

Then a child spoke: "Mom . . . do you want a Band-Aid?" It was the child who thinks Band-Aids are some kind of a reward and will cure anything.

"When do you plan to come out?" The husband spoke again.

"I have no plans for the immediate future."

"Is there anything we can do?" He was beginning to sound kind of pathetic himself, so I took some time to think about that one. Then I said feebly, "Well, I was thinking a cup of hot chocolate . . ."

"You've got it!" he said as he raced off toward the kitchen.

Now, I'm embarrassed for you to know that I ever got that pitiful. But I had to tell you that story in order to tell you this: When I came out of my bedroom, my family was waiting with open arms. I might as well have used the same words my tiny nephew spoke when he said, "Me need you." They loved me back together again. When you have a family like that, you can never be "poor 'n' pitiful." You might get pitiful once in awhile, but believe me, you can never be poor.

When you have that kind of love—and a cup of hot chocolate and a box of Band-Aids—you've got just about everything.

The Reason for the January Blahs

I must confess to having an occasional pitiful spell during the month of January. It has nothing to do with the weather or the after-Christmas blahs or being sick. It has to do with the mail.

The mail we get in January would depress Mrs. Santa Claus. Every January our mailbox is stuffed full of something called "the family newsletter." These are glowing accounts of families that enjoy major expeditions to the East Indies without having a cross word and of husbands who have conquered new horizons within the twelve months since their last public manifesto.

The children of these high achievers have also somehow managed to inherit only the best qualities of their parents and—you guessed it—are high achievers too. These children can be adopted, will "still" aspire to go to M.I.T., and will be the next generation to discover some miracle cure for which there is no known illness.

It's never enough to stop with the scholastic achievements of these former ankle biters. The authors of these masterpieces give glowing details of social accomplishments, contests won, and civic honors that could merit citizen-of-the-year eight times in a row.

By comparison, my own family staggers through the year like a person needing a huge dose of vitamin B_{12}. Our children must be the only ones whose career choices in life include the foreign legion or fighting local fires with the family hose pipe.

It took a lot of courage, but one afternoon as our youngest returned from school, I asked the "big" question: "Have you ever considered M.I.T.?"

He said, "Well, I did want a new one a while back, but I'm not much into baseball anymore."

So much for M.I.T.!

The only club he's ever belonged to was the one we took away from him because he used it on a neighbor's little boy one day.

He is concerned about community affairs, though. He bought a police scanner so that he could be on the local rescue squad and be a volunteer firefighter. He slept through all the calls and had his membership revoked.

Those newsletters make every mom and dad sound like a Ken and Barbie who have finally married and produced pristine little offspring, who go through life without so much as getting smudges on their faces. They probably have BMW stamped on their behinds.

These children have skipped right past diapers and have never thrown up a day in their lives. But if they were to be sick, they would be self-cleaning. It makes me sick just thinking about it.

The parents give "coming out" parties for their daughters. The only time we felt it necessary to have a coming out party was when someone finally came out of the bathroom after turning thirteen.

We're just ordinary people who do ordinary things and laugh about them. We've had children stay in the bathroom so long we put a glass to the door to check for any sign of life. As long as we could hear a page turn now and then, we knew everything was fine. Can you imagine reading that in a family newsletter?

Some of these letters contain pictures—just in case you don't believe what you read. You can see for yourself how great they look wearing designer smiles. These pictures are most often taken in front of the fireplace. Hanging on the hearth are Victorian stockings that would bankrupt Santa if he tried to fill them. All the little names of all the little people are emblazoned in gold leaf on the fronts. Why, just re- membering the tube socks I hung on the mantel one year brings a tear to my eye.

Every time I read one of those letters, I consider putting myself up for adoption. But they tell me there isn't much action for forty-year-old women who cry a lot.

We received one photograph of a family who all had their legs crossed in the same direction at the same time. In our family if we wanted to achieve something like that, we'd have to break the legs first.

Just last Christmas we tried getting the entire family together in the same room for a family photo. The result might have been an award winner if "Family Feud" was still on TV, but it will never make it onto a Christmas card.

Sometimes the pictures of these other families were taken during the heat of the previous summer when their tans were deep and rich. They are stand- ing in front of the family flower bed, which looks as if the Jolly Green Giant just visited and sprinkled quick grow on every living thing. The flower pots out front aren't plastic from K-Mart; they are burst- ing forth with plants to prove what the family told you in the letter about having studied horticulture together that year and that they actually practice it on weekends—together.

Our family doesn't have a green thumb among us. We have been known to have green between our toes, but I've yet to discover if anything thrives in it besides sock fuzz.

I'm considering composing my own family newsletter to send to these people just to expose them to a small dose of reality. I will tell them that one of our family's major accomplishments this year was simply getting a term paper turned in on time. I will tell them that our youngest son actually learned to take his keys out of the door instead of leaving them on the outside for the convenience of would-be burglars. And I will fill some space by telling them that on three days last year the laundry was caught up, the dog got a bath, and we had a home cooked meal.

I could tell them how long it takes to vacuum up five pounds of flour from the kitchen floor. And stimulate them with the news that one of the boys now wears tennis shoes so big that I could put petunias in them and put them out on the front porch as planters. I will surely tell them that we have a son who works at a seafood restaurant and comes home smelling like the bottom of a shrimp boat.

Our year is so packed full of endless accomplishments that if I wrote a family newsletter, I wouldn't be able to afford the postage to mail it.

While you may look ordinary on paper, it is not so bad. Most of life is a series of repetitions of ordinary events. You can perform most of them in your sleep, but stay awake anyway. If you doze off you might miss something.

7

THE SECRET
OF SERENDIPITY
(Ordinary "Fun")

I am acquainted with many couples, like my own parents, who have been married for a long time, many of them forty-plus years.

The longevity of these marriages has proven several existing theories: one, that opposites attract; two, that you can stay married for life in spite of theory number one; and three, that no matter how long you remain married, you will remain opposites.

Knowing all these long-time couples has disproven the old saying that "the longer you stay married, the more you look alike." If this were true, some of us would be in big trouble. This old saying had me worried for years. Just think about it. Would you like the idea of waking up one morning looking just like your spouse? And can you imagine going home to visit your parents only to find that you can't tell them apart?

This opposites business has a long-term effect on the family. It's like this—opposites attract, and that's how you get a family that can't agree on anything. My childhood family was a classic in the opposites department. Daddy always wanted us to face reality; Momma wanted us to have fun. When you bring children into a family like that, those opposites get in there and crisscross. The next thing you know, you

111

have people who can never make up their minds about anything; they just keep changing them.

One Person's Great Idea Is Torture to Another

When you begin the search for common "fun" to do together as a family, you find that children can be more opposite than their parents. You can have one child who would prefer to live in the local pet store. She'll want to bring home creatures that are no longer found in nature or that live under rocks.

Then, sure as the world, you'll have another child who is allergic to fur, birdseed, bark, and practically everything else that the rest of you hold dear. We had a child like that. He itched his way through eight states and six grades of school. His teachers were really fond of him. He was eight before people knew his name. It was, "Oh, yes, the one with the rash."

Once, by some miracle, we agreed to go on a picnic. We had just opened up the food when the boy who was into insects sat down on a mountain of red ants. They crawled up his shorts and visited places no one but family had ever seen before. He's normally a very modest child, but for some reason that day he didn't care who was watching.

He was coming out of clothes like a quick-change artist. So, we packed up the picnic lunch and went home.

We used to go to local softball games as a family. My husband and I thought we were doing this for the children. We watched people we had never met play softball while the children played under the bleachers and collected stuff other people had thrown away. One of these children has a master's degree in junk. If our local city ever finds out how much he likes junk, he will probably get an offer to solve the city's landfill problem. If they wait long enough, there won't be a problem; all the trash will already be in his room.

Our family also likes to play games together. When you play games with three children, you're talking major fun. One of them is always "right," one of them is always "wrong," and the other one changes all the rules. You need an attorney, an accountant, a member of the rescue squad, and a judge to settle the score.

Some of the best "fun" we've had together as a family came from these very ordinary times as we sat around in the floor together, argued over who was really winning, laughed at knock-knock jokes that somebody made up on the spot, and just being silly in general. Those were rich times, and I wouldn't take anything for them.

These kinds of activities allow children to express themselves, to be right, to be wrong, and to drive parents half crazy.

As I reflect on those days, I am impressed by how many of our family stories—those favorite stories—come from the times we were down on the floor playing together and developing the skill of blending our differences. They are great memories but just plain, simple, and wonderfully ordinary.

Most true fun is hidden in the very ordinary places of our lives. For years I waited for something extraordinary to happen. I tried to make fun happen by planning activities that took me away from the everydayness of my life. I eventually discovered that expecting the extraordinary, the spectacular, to occur went totally against the entire concept of experiencing serendipity in life.

Serendipity is the joy of the unexpected, and because it is unexpected, it cannot be planned. I believe my mother taught me this, and only now do I fully understand it. Like most of us, she didn't have the option of looking for something spectacular to bring joy into her life. She looks for and finds joy from something that occurs while life is merely turning another ordinary page of another ordinary day.

If she's canning vegetables until she feels like a stalk of broccoli, she'll have a "your-father-and-'his'-garden" story to tell us. If one of the grandbabies comes to visit, she calls with a "you-won't-believe-what-Steven-said-today" story. She makes life a joy by perceiving it as a joy day by day by day.

Mashed Potatoes Will Never Be the Same

Years ago—probably centuries ago—some woman with nothing better to do determined that food should be passed in one direction only around the table. She decided which direction that was, and families have been disagreeing about it ever since.

Our family only disagreed about it every time we had company for dinner, which was fairly often. Half the food would start around in one direction, and half would go in the other direction; then Momma would inform us we were going in the wrong direction. All the food would pause and go back where it came from. It was very confusing.

But we loved having people to dinner anyway because every now and then it would be the guest who would provide us with the unexpected—like the man who had a sneezing spell. When he let out his final sneeze, his false teeth parted company with his mouth and landed right side up in the mashed potato bowl.

This definitely qualified for the unexpected—so much so that no one knew what to do next, except stare at the mashed potato bowl in disbelief. Momma got up and left the room to go into the kitchen and pinch herself. The poor, toothless man didn't even know what to do. I mean, would you know what to do if your teeth were grinning up at you from a pile of mashed potatoes?

The man didn't look very good, but you should have seen his wife. She looked worse than he did. One of my brothers finally broke the ice. He said, "Would anybody like some more mashed potatoes?" No one did.

The Last Time We Saw Him
He Was Headed That-a-Way

The joy of the unexpected can happen when you get two or more children together.

When two children get together and agree on something, you have a gang. That's how I happened to find myself in the woods with three boys, five horses, and a husband who was down on his knees begging, "Just shoot me in the leg—anything, please—just don't make me get on this animal!"

You can see how excited he was about horseback riding. He was tear-gassed in the sixties while covering a riot for the news media, and *that* is a fonder memory than his last encounter with anything that gets around on four legs and lives on oats.

I tried to tell him there was nothing to it, that he could do anything he set his mind to.

He said, "Sure, I can set my mind to it . . . it's the other parts of my body that are begging for mercy!" When we finally talked him onto the mare's back, he muttered, "She just doesn't look right to me. She just cut her eyes back at me and snorted 'sucker' through those fat lips of hers." He was having so much fun.

Finally, all five of us were mounted up and ready to ride into the sunset—with at least one of us convinced he was riding off to his final resting place.

Those same children who had promised to "stay with the family, keep together till the end of the trail," and all that other stuff none of them meant, were gone in a flash with the sound of "Ride 'em, cowboy" hanging thickly in the air. I was guilty of joining in the fun and of feeling superior in the situation.

In the next moment, I came to realize that superiority is a dangerous attitude—especially when it is straddling a horse snorting fire. I had no sooner pronounced the words, "Just follow me," when my horse whinnied once, clicked his heels, and ground my superiority to a pulp.

This fella had undoubtedly been expelled from the Kentucky Derby for quick starting. He took off so fast it would have made Roy Rogers dizzy. That animal was determined to give me blisters in the place where I was supposed to have cellulite. When I finally gathered both my wits at the same time, I remembered to yank up sharply on the reins and hold. The animal trotted to a stop somewhere just shy of too late.

That gave me my first opportunity to look behind me. A cloud of dust was just beginning to come into focus when I recognized him. And that was when the surprise of the unexpected hit me. I had shared nearly everything with this man for years, but had no idea he could ride upside down under the belly of a horse and change his last will and testament simultaneously!

I followed him down the trail trying to picture life without him. Every now and then his screams reached me, and a particular word kept standing out. It was that other word for a donkey—I didn't even know it was part of his vocabulary, but under the circumstances, he was hardly to blame.

We came to an abrupt halt at the end of the trail. When the children laid eyes on their daddy, they burst into shrieks of laughter that made birds fly out of trees. "Stop it! Stop it this instant, boys! This is no laughing matter—I mean it!" I threatened.

They were heartless. "Look at him!" they said between throes of hysteria. "I never saw anybody ride under there before except at the rodeo." (Laughter) "Yeah, but they did it on purpose!" (More laughter)

I slid off the back of my horse and walked cautiously over to my husband. By this time, the boys had used up all their one-liners, dismounted, and sauntered over to stand beside me.

"What's he doing under there?" the youngest one said.

"Is he breathing?" the oldest asked, obviously realizing the seriousness of the situation and that he had just been written out of all future wills. After all, this expedition was his idea.

"Do we need to do the Heimlich maneuver on him?"

"Hush!" I ordered. "That's for someone who's choking to death. Which, if your father is still alive, is exactly what he may do to you."

"Darlin'," I said gently, "you can let go now. It's all over. We're right beside you. No one's going to hurt you." It was a lot like talking someone down from an eighteen-story ledge—but he was only six inches from the ground.

His eyes looked as if they'd been surgically glued together, and his hands had developed something like lockjaw. They were dug into that horse flesh so deep that when we finally talked him into letting go, he was clutching a wad of horse hair big enough to stuff a pillow.

It took all four of us to stand him upright, and for once the boys did the right thing—absolutely nothing! My husband stood up, put his arm around my shoulder, and said, "I never understood that movie before."

"What movie?"

"You know—*They Shoot Horses, Don't They?*"

We never used that "fun" idea again, but recalling it is on our list of favorite things to do.

Truckload of Sod and Other Fun

The word *fun* has an unlimited number of definitions to different people. Some folks think skiing with their families is fun. My husband hates anything that makes a chill run down his spine. Some people pray for summer to come early so they can bake their tiny little bodies to a well-done crisp. Humidity and summer heat make my feet swell, my head ache, and my attitude go downhill fast, so that's not my idea of fun.

Our son told us that school was not fun. We said, "If we'd wanted you to have fun, we'd have enrolled you in Disney World."

My sister-in-law decided it would be "fun" to have my brother dig up a large portion of their back yard for a flower bed. My brother has been married just barely long enough to recognize that whatever she's decided is fun, he'd better decide is fun too. That makes for a good marriage. Then he goes about getting the entire family involved in having some fun.

He said, "Come on, boys. We're going to dig up some dirt and make Momma a flower bed."

Anything to do with dirt is fun to boys. It doesn't matter how old or how many degrees they have before or after their names; they will still love dirt. After all, a boy is "just a noise with dirt on it." You can whisper the word *dirt* to a two-day-old male child, and he will quit crying and burp on cue.

My brother dug up the back yard in an orderly fashion, into squares of sod. Sod is just a fancy name for dirt with the grass still growing on top of it.

Diplomacy was born in a family just like this one. When my brother gets a hair-brained idea that he thinks is "fun," he's figured out that the best way to accomplish it—over his wife's frazzled body—is to get the boys "all fired up," as my sister-in-law puts it. Once those little fellas are charged up, no matter how crazy the idea is, how could she say no?

On this occasion, while the mother of these little boys was at the grocery store, my brother said, "Boys, we could make some money off this dirt! This is great sod. . . . Somebody would buy this, boys."

"Wet's do it, Daddy," said the four-year-old entrepreneur.

" 'Es Daddy," chimed in the two-and-a-half-year-old. (He has no earthly idea what "it" is—he's just "fired up.")

By now you have some idea what my dear sister-in-law is up against. Every now and then I send her a sympathy card for all she puts up with—and for how beautifully she manages the men in her life. She says, "Me, manage? You must be kidding. I haven't had a moment's control since my last Lamaze class!"

Well, when the sod was loaded into the back of my brother's army M.A.S.H. truck, he backed it up to the edge of the driveway and parked it in front of the whole world—complete with a huge sign, hand painted with the words, "Truckload of Delicious Sod . . . $40.00."

The four-year-old said, "Daddy, how will we know if somebody wants to buy it?" and "Don't we need to sit out there wiff it?" (The little fella's *th* sounds are still in the making.)

The mother and wife of all this "fun" may not have any control, but she's got perfect timing. She came zipping down the street and came to a screeching halt before the driveway. That was where she was faced with a life-changing decision—to keep on driving or to turn in. She turned in.

She was taking in groceries muttering loudly enough for all the boys to hear, "I've never been so embarrassed in all my life."

The four-year-old was beating a path between the kitchen and the truck saying, "Daddy, why is Momma embarrassed? . . . What's wrong, Momma, don't you wike my dirt?" He couldn't figure out why she didn't think their dirt was fun.

Business began to pick up. When a man stopped to inquire about the sod but didn't buy, four-year-old Tyler was deeply offended.

"Why didn't the man want to buy our dirt, Daddy?" The free enterprise system is not easy to explain when the subject is dirt. When the asking price came down, the next man who stopped bought the sod. And that's how it came about that a four-year-old sold a truckload of "delicious sod."

The money didn't mean a thing to the two-year-old. He was blissfully rolling around in the hole in the ground where the sod had been. There was no fight over splitting the profits.

Later that evening, my sister-in-law saw a great teaching opportunity. With the next day being Sunday and all, she proceeded to talk with Tyler about his newly acquired wealth—how everything we have comes from God, how since the next day was to be Sunday, we always give back to God a little bit of what we make.

You've heard the expression "that went over like a lead balloon?" Well, feel free to apply it here. That whole idea ruffled his tiny little bank book. He said, "Uh-uh! Momma, I just got my money." (He was looking at her as if she had just proposed selling his baby brother.) "No, Momma, I just got my money, and I do not fink . . . I do not fink God would want me to have to give it back!"

Now, you tell me, does God smile every now and then? Yep! He smiles—at a daddy spending time to make work seem like play and at a momma taking time to make play a time for teaching—whether it takes or not!

There's a time for work, a time for play, a time for teaching, a time for laughter—and frequently, the four go together.

The Secret of Serendipity

I don't know if there's a secret to developing this spirit within a family. If there is, it lies within that God-given joy in the hearts of people who love each other. It lies within the desire to believe the best of each other and desire the best for each other. It lies within a certain acceptable kind of pride in saying, "This is my family . . . all of them. They're mine and I am theirs."

Families are not people stamped out by some kind of genetic cookie cutter. We're all unique, different from each other. So if there is a secret to being a family that remains a family for life, it is in the commitment to staying in touch and to loving our families, flaws and all. It is in the love that endures disappointments, sickness, poverty, the passage of time, horseback rides, and sticky kisses.

I've known of families that put love of money or a family business or a myriad of other temporal "things" above love for each other. There's no real profit in those families, for in the pursuit of financial gain, they become colossal losers—along the way, they lose each other. My family has been lucky. The only business we're involved in together is "monkey business."

Someone recently asked First Lady Barbara Bush how in this era of out-of-touch families, she manages to stay in such close, almost intimate contact with her grown children and extended family. She said, "No matter how busy we are, we see to it that everyone is always welcome. . . . We encourage our children to bring their children and their friends home, to share their friends with us."

She ended the comment with, "You have to love your children unselfishly." As I read between the lines of what she said and what she didn't say, I'll add that the basis for that kind of staying in touch is the love that first of all breeds the *desire* to stay in touch.

Times have changed, and we can probably count on their continuing to change. So it's up to us to seek out the little pieces of life that will become our children's memories, the small treasures in their adult lives. We do that by making life special in the smallest, the simplest, the most meaningful ways.

Think back, recall, and pull out of your family's history those wonderfully ordinary times, and decide to see them as some of the best "fun" you've ever had.

In fact, this may be what the complicated families of today are desperately searching for and are overlooking in the noise of constant activity, packed calendars, dual careers, and too little time.

When you learn to look for and find joy within the tedium of life, you may have discovered the secret of being content in whatever your circumstances. Instead of waiting for and dreaming of the spectacular, you begin now to notice the little things, little moments, and place the proper value on them.

Some of those moments for me are a family breakfast together, the smell of coffee brewing, and the anticipation of morning talk around the steaming mugs of that first cup. In our family, whoever is available—sometimes women, sometimes one of our husbands—will join Momma in the kitchen to scramble eggs, fry sausage, and pour juice. There's nothing unique about it. Nothing *Better Homes and Gardens* would consider an elegant family tradition. The only ingredient making these times memorable is the people who honestly love each other doing some mundane task like cooking breakfast—together. There's always a grandchild who wants to help and a grandmother who lets him. We walk all over each other, but no one seems to notice.

The TV gets turned on by one person and immediately turned off by another. Daddy can never find his glasses or his shoes, and somebody is always either too hot, too cold, too loud, or too dirty.

It's just a family staying close.

Sometimes we stumble over the most obvious treasure while we're going about the ordinary. We fail to see the humor that is happening right in the middle of it.

This realization was brought home to me one day when I ran out to buy bags for my vacuum cleaner. I rushed into my local discount store behind a woman who had four children dangling from all parts of her body, along with a handbag, a diaper bag, and a shell-shocked look on her face. She was grabbing moving targets that resembled children from all directions and stuffing them in the cart like sale items—she had more than her share. When the cart was full of the moving targets, there wasn't any room for her to do any shopping.

I figured she didn't have any shopping to do anyway. She just needed to be in the presence of some adult-type people. She needed the assurance that there were people left in the world who didn't want something to eat or need something changed and who wouldn't spit up on her.

I followed her for a few aisles in amazement. I'd never seen a woman pushing an octopus before. There were arms and legs going in every direction, grabbing items, and trying to poke them into each other's mouths.

I left her somewhere between toys and automotive supplies. I admit to feeling a little sorry for her, yet I was envious at the same time. I was sorry for her because the long-suffering look on her face and her tone of voice revealed that she had absolutely *no* idea how much fun she was having. Those children will be half grown before she realizes some of the funny moments they've given her. While she may never wish to relive those days, she will want to recall with fondness and humor those arms and legs wrapping themselves around her.

I was a tiny bit envious because I'm just barely old enough to know that almost any moment, and very often our most difficult moments in life, can turn out to be treasured ones. I recognized her moment—that of pushing four babies in a cart.

Children give you so many opportunities to appreciate the ordinary that you may not be able to move fast enough to keep up with them.

8

THIS FAMILY
HAS A FEW LOOSE
ENDS, AND THEY'RE
ALL UNDER AGE
(Living with Children)

You can always identify the mothers at a grocery store. They are the women who fall asleep on top of their carts in the checkout lane. You can always find the mothers when you're stopped at a red light. They fall asleep on the steering wheel if the light takes too long. If they are awake, they will be turned completely around in their seats talking to someone nobody else can even see.

You can even tell which women have raised children somewhere in the distant past. If you're riding in the car with one and she has to brake suddenly, she'll fling her body over yours to keep you from hitting the dash.

Mothers are not retrainable. They are women who will spend their lives trying to burp inanimate objects and bracing themselves before opening a bedroom door. They are women who try to live normal lives. They do things like go shopping, and when a sales clerk says, "May I help you?" the mother will say, "Ask your father!"

A mother is someone who is afraid to stick her hands down in her children's pockets. And she isn't crazy about looking under beds.

You know you're a mother when you begin to understand everything the family dog says.

You know you're a mother when you have a recurring dream that you are the agitator in a washing machine and you're off balance.

You know beyond a shadow of a doubt that you're a mother when one of your top-ten fears is that there will be carpooling in heaven.

You are surely a mother if you have actually tried to save a stitch in time but have long since given up.

A mother is someone who talks in her sleep, but no one listens.

You know you're a mother when you buy cereal based on what kind of picture is on the box and what kind of "surprise" is *in* the box.

You know you're a father if your wife fits any of the above descriptions.

You know you're a father if you feel neglected once in a while.

You know you're a father if you find a Mutant Ninja Turtle in your briefcase and you take it around the office for "Show and Tell."

You know you're a father if you find a clean house when you come home from work and think you must be in the wrong one.

You know you're a father when you take a client to lunch and automatically ask for a booster seat.

You know you're a father when you put your wife in the back seat and fasten her seat belt for her.

You know you're a father when you keep fighting the urge to wipe somebody's mouth with your shirttail.

And you know you're a parent if the only thing you know about the sun is that it gets here too early in the morning.

You know you're a parent if you're tired. Parents who don't get tired must be doing something wrong.

I recently read a magazine article which included some hints for tired moms. I think the title of the article was redundant. The name *mom* is synonymous with tired. This article said that periodically during the day to relieve stress, a tired mom should stop everything, place a hand on her stomach, breathe in deeply, arch her back, raise her shoulders, *and* wrinkle up her facial muscles.

I felt tired just reading it. I don't know about you, but I'm not sure that I can move that many body parts at the same time. Just imagine it. If you tried doing this every time you felt stressed out, you'd be going around patting your stomach and breathing like an asthmatic nearly all day long.

Not to mention the fact that I have *never* met a woman, tired or otherwise, who wanted an exercise that helped her to wrinkle her face!

I think it would be a great disservice to mothers to eliminate tiredness from parenting. If you weren't tired at the end of the day, you probably wouldn't fall asleep before your head hits the pillow anymore. If you couldn't have the privilege of being tired, you wouldn't be able to appreciate taking naps when you get old. Being tired is a badge of honor to a parent, and it should be worn with pride and hope—the hope that someday you will be allowed to sleep uninterrupted and that when you wake you will know where you are and no one will be calling your name.

The Child Who Has Everything
Will Lose It Come Sunday Morning

Child rearing is meant to keep you on your toes. It's like an unchoreographed ballet. Just when you think you have everything figured out, something changes. At the very moment you begin to fear that your children will never even like each other, they begin to be nice to each other. That is a high moment for any parent, to know that your children really love each other and can do nice things for one another. That's when Sunday morning will come around, and you learn something else about your children.

They do not like to be nice to each other on Sunday morning. This is a special and important day of the week because hopefully you're getting ready to go to church. You are supposed to be doing it while singing, whistling, and humming a bar of "Amazing Grace."

But this will be the morning some person in the family wakes up in a mood that would cause an optimist to go belly up. No matter what you do, it's wrong—too late, too early, or smells funny.

If you manage to prepare hot food, your family won't go near it. They say, "Mom, you know I can't eat this early in the morning." Of course you know that; you were just practicing for the Betty Crocker cook-off. Or another child will say, "Mom, I *can't* eat! I've already brushed my teeth"—like tooth brushing is an act which can only be committed once on Sunday.

I'm telling you, getting a family ready for church on Sunday should carry hazardous duty pay. There's an unseen enemy telling everyone to make a scene, cry, lose clothes, or pick a fight.

We had one child who cried every Sunday because he wanted to take candy to eat in Sunday school. This was the same child who believed M&M's were one of the four basic food groups.

On Sunday morning, a child with a usually sunny disposition will begin to cry, point to another child who is in a bad mood about to be made worse, and say, "He did it! He took . . . my Bible . . . [sob-sob] He took my Bible and . . . now . . . [more sobbing] I can't go to church ever again in my whole life!"

You locate the missing Bible and put it in the hands of its rightful owner. Then somebody else points an accusing finger and says, "You didn't take a bath last night—I saw what you did. You just turned on the shower and never got in it. You just stood there reading a comic book, and *that's* why you smell like a goat." This is why children can be *so* popular with each other.

Everything That Goes Around Comes Around If You Live Long Enough

I now understand what my parents were up against. The only way I could miss church when I was growing up was to have a signed death certificate; and even then Momma wanted two witnesses.

When I was a child, I wasn't crazy about the words "Are you ready yet?", "Hurry up," and "We're going to be late." Now those phrases are part of my own vocabulary.

I still remember being fifteen, so I *know* stuff that our children don't realize I know. I know that when a fifteen-year-old says, "Just a minute," it means that he is nowhere close to being ready yet and that we are going to be very late. You can plan ahead, you can even start early, and a teenager will use up all the extra time plus some. In fact, if your family is like ours, you have to start early to be as late as we've been most of our lives.

You just mention the possibility of being late to my husband, and the hair on top of his head becomes airborne.

Children and teenagers don't understand the concept of being early. They think that early is when the sun comes up, and everything that happens after that is meant to be late. This is one of the major causes of stress among families everywhere—that and getting socks to match.

I'm starting a self-help group for people who have to sort the socks for an entire family. We will use the twelve steps of sorting, which I will be making up as we go along, just as I do every time I do the laundry.

I Don't Know What It Is, But It Must Be a Nice One

Stress can come from practically any direction after you have children. You wouldn't have it any other way; it lets you know you are still alive. To experience stress is to be fully alive. It's your response to the stress that makes life interesting.

Sometimes just when you think you have all your loose ends gathered up into nice little packages, when you think you have all your bases covered, another loose end will fly up in your face. This happened in our family the day our children began to look forward to the arrival of the mail carrier every day. I began to receive bills for things I had never seen, much less ordered.

All a teenager has to see at the top of a beautifully designed mail order ad is, "Order absolutely free . . . under 'no' obligation to pay!" and zippitty-do-dah, off goes the form. Teenagers are characteristically shortsighted and cannot read below the bold type to the crux of the matter, which in business terms means the bottom line which says, "Pay in 30 days, or we will send a 400-pound Sumo wrestler into your home to shorten your legs."

One of the surprises waiting for me at the mailbox one morning was a do-it-yourself kit for setting your broken bones in the privacy of your own bathroom. This sounded like an idea made in Alcatraz. So I ended up paying for the do-it-yourself kit; I've seen those Sumo wrestlers on television and didn't want to take any chances.

I finally decided the only way to end the mail order mania around our house was to be the first person to get the mail every day. Our mail order monster came in and asked me what I had done with the mail, like I was guilty of eating it.

I said, "Listen, just because your report cards come in the mail, and just because your dad and I have to park our bodies in sleeping bags out on the front lawn waiting for the mail carrier every six weeks to keep the report card from 'getting lost in the mail,' is no reason to get defensive about the mail."

This child ordered records before he had a job to pay for them. He ordered five hundred minnows to start his own fish bait farm. They were dead on arrival. The mail carrier wrote me a nice little note over that one. Once, this boy joined a top-forty tape club before he even owned a tape player.

He wanted to order some baby chickens for a science project. I told him that would be fine if he planned to live at the school until the chickens graduated and went off to college. The mail order mania finally came to an end the day he discovered girls. But I never did figure out what to do with the fourteen-foot-long inflatable airplane that came in the mail last summer.

Thank Goodness for Little Girls

All children develop and mature at their own unique pace. My friends and I were discussing this very mysterious fact one day when one friend said that her youngest boy's hormones came in when he was three months old. He only smiled, burped, or slept when he was in the arms of a female person. She said he was the only child in nursery school going steady.

Our boys weren't like that, thank goodness. They were slow bloomers, and for that we'll always be grateful. When one of the boys was thirteen, we wanted to give him a birthday party. So I asked him to make out a list of friends he wanted to invite. He handed me a list containing the names of ten boys.

I said, "Wouldn't you like to invite more of a balanced group?"

"Like what?" he said.

"Like a few girls. Wouldn't you like to invite a few girls?"

His eyes sort of bumped into each other in the middle of his nose, and he said, "You mean *girls?*" Then he yelled, "Aarugh!" the way somebody would yell shark at the beach while running for dear life.

The next year he handed me a list for his fourteenth birthday party. It contained the names of two boys and eight girls. I said, "Son, don't you think you should invite more of a balanced group?"

He said, "It looks like a perfectly balanced group to me," and left the room. That was the year he stopped waiting for the mail to come.

Experimenting with the Family Car

When my husband was teaching one of his sons how to drive, they both came back home in a bad mood every time. I don't care if you're the most patient parent since Grandma Moses, you'll discover that you can walk to the edge of madness while you're teaching a teenager to drive.

A fifteen-year-old boy with a permit thinks he already knows everything he has been begging you to teach him. If he narrowly misses an eighty-year-old grandmother crossing the street, he has everything under control. A teenager has extraordinary skill behind the wheel. If there is only one pothole anywhere within a three-mile radius of your home, he will go out of his way to find it and hit it.

A teenage daughter will want to practice applying makeup in the rearview mirror as soon as she pulls out of the driveway for the first time. And a stop sign is not a mark of a dangerous intersection where you stop to watch for oncoming traffic; it is a place where you have one more chance to look at yourself in the mirror.

Our son was so busy checking the oncoming cars for someone he recognized that he nearly rear-ended a truckload of horses.

Teenagers believe that the first thing you have to check out when you get behind the wheel is a radio station. They find it next to impossible to put the car in drive until their favorite music is turned up to feedback level.

Living with a teenager who's experimenting with the family car is scary for parents. They will try out things like making two-wheel stops, splitting the atom, breaking the sound barrier, and whiplash takeoffs.

When our last son was going through this stage, my husband pretended to be nonchalant. When I fretted, he would say, "Just relax, the boy's going to be fine—just fine! This is perfectly normal. We'll survive."

I said, "This boy's been driving crazy ever since he discovered we live in the same town as that Darrell Waltrip guy who won the Daytona 500."

"You're overreacting as usual," he told me. "How fast can you go in a ten-year-old, five-speed Datsun that needs a new transmission?" He pretended to be so cool about it, but one Saturday night I found him hiding behind a shrub out front trying to see the boy's takeoffs and landings.

When a child gets even temporary possession of anything on four wheels, he is never the same again. My little nephews both went through a personality change when they got their first car. It came in a kit and ran on flashlight batteries.

This boy of ours sits in his car like he's trying to hatch something. He's got stereo equipment all over his bedroom, but would rather listen to his $39.95 car tape deck. Two teenage boys will take a tape deck and a twelve-volt battery and sit in a burned-out car in a junk yard before they'll listen to a full-blown quadraphonic sound system in the house.

This car business affected our entire family. We were forced to change our meal times because our son was always out in the car. I was forced to offer curb service. We set food outside the driver's side door three times a day whether he needed it or not. I know he was taking in nourishment because he wrote a note and left it on the food tray. It said, "Mom, don't send spaghetti anymore; it doesn't look too good on my new lamb's wool seat covers."

One day when the phone rang, my husband took the call and walked to his closet to grab a coat before heading for the door.

"What is it? What's happening?" I asked, grabbing my own coat while I followed him.

"That was our son," he said. "Seems the drive shaft fell off his car. He's stranded out on the parkway."

"What's a drive shaft?" I asked. "Did he wear it out from sitting on it too much?" Then I said, "This is wonderful! He needs us again! Do you think you'll recognize him when you see him?"

We had our son back for a week while the car was in the shop. It was like getting to know him all over again. Having a vehicle is such a mind-expanding experience. He had so much more to share with us. I kept the auto manual close at hand so I could look up terms like piston and spark something-or-others. The day they drove the car home from the shop, the boy and his dad came in the back door together. The boy was smiling; the father was not. I walked out to say hello, just in time to catch the cloud of smoke going down the street.

"There he goes," I said.

"Umhumph!" my husband said. "And the next time you see him, he may have a wife and three children."

"Naw," I said. "There's not a woman alive who'd live in *that* car!"

Term Paper in the Dryer

Nobody told me that the family laundry room could be the scene of so many disasters. I just figured it out by going from crisis to crisis—all by myself. This is probably why I have a recurring dream that I am the agitator in a washing machine and that I'm off balance.

We have a son who is no good at hiding things. He's forgetful. Everything he picks up or finds or needs later, he stashes in the pocket of some garment that will ultimately find its way to the washing machine. I've spent so much time piecing together mysterious papers and unidentifiable objects that I may have a future career as an FBI investigator.

In the years this child's been around, I've taken enough shredded paper out of the lint filter to have a ticker tape parade for the shuttle astronauts. It's no longer a great mystery as to why there are "incompletes" on this person's report cards. (This boy believes that an "incomplete" means he has all the time he wants to "think" about doing the work.) All this boy's work disintegrates in the dryer, and it's my job to put it back together.

One day after piecing together a few of the shreds of paper, I said, "Son, what's a term paper doing in the washing machine?"

He said, "Well, Mom, it wasn't my fault." (I could see his mental wheels cranking at seventy-eight rpm and was beginning to smell rubber burning.)

"Well, I was walking home from school, and as I turned a corner, this big truck . . . no, I mean, it was a dog, a big dog . . . this big dog came out from behind a bush. It was a big bush. And . . . this dog . . . you just wouldn't believe it . . . headed right for my notebook. That's right, my notebook . . . the one with my term paper in it. . . . So . . . well . . . after the attack was over, I picked up what was left of my term paper and put it in my pocket. So I guess that's how my term paper got in the dryer!"

In fact, we've been a little concerned about career choices around our house. Have you ever noticed that when you ask preschoolers what they want to be when they grow up, they always have an answer on the tip of their tongues? I bent down over a friend's little three-year-old son and asked him the big question. I said, "And what do you want to be when you grow up?"

His eyes lit up and he said, "A firefly?"

"Oh, you want to be a fire fighter?" I said, thinking I was correctly interpreting his three-year-old speech. Wrong!

Shaking his head from side to side, he said again, "Uhn-uh, a firefly."

Well, I thought he was about to make a serious career mistake, but he was only three and probably had time to be a firefly, a bumblebee, a bullfrog, or just about anything else he wanted to be.

But when your "children" become eighteen, you begin to get a little concerned about their future. In fact, if you want to know the truth, you can start being concerned a lot earlier than that. When you ask an eighteen-year-old what he wants to be or to study in college, he will clear his throat several times then ask you to repeat the question.

But after the term-paper-in-the-dryer incident, we stopped worrying. We felt sure that with his experience in shredding papers and with his creative imagination, there will always be a job for him somewhere . . . a government job maybe?

A Sister's Chore in Life

The relationship between siblings is a wonderful source of joy, wonder, and mystery, and it's an endless source of humor to me. Many times in the middle of dealing with something in my immediate family, my mind flashes back to a particular incident from my childhood family. Those memories have served as a comfort to me, as an encouragement, and have helped me to look for the laughter in every corner of my life—and I usually find it. Memories of my childhood family help me to be more patient with my immediate family . . . sometimes.

When you have more than one child, you learn that each child assumes a different role in the family. An older sister's role in life is to take care of all the other children. And she achieves this by running straight to Momma the second one of the siblings gets within a hairbreadth of trouble. This, as you know, makes her very popular with the parents but a sore spot in the side of all the other siblings.

This was my job when I was growing up, and everybody knew it.

"Momma . . ." I said breathlessly, "they're doing it!"

"What?"

"Jim and Rodney—they're standing too close to it!"

"Too close to *what?*" she asked.

"The fire! Daddy's burning trash, and they're standing out there throwing sticks into it—sticks and everything else they can find!"

Momma pondered that bit of information before answering.

Good, I thought. *Now I'm getting somewhere.*

"Just tell them to be careful," she said.

"Humph!" I said disappointedly. *She's not even going to get excited, and that's supposed to be what she does best,* I thought. (My momma could get excited watching the shift change at the GM plant.)

I stomped down the back porch steps and out to the scene of the fire, put on my best sisterly, you-better-listen-to-me-voice, and yelled, "Momma said you better be careful or else!"

I noticed they were already standing a good distance farther from the flames. They wouldn't even look at me, and that really got under my skin. Never one to be ignored, I pranced right up to those little fellas and tried again.

"Momma said, you'd better be—"

Jim butted in before the words were out of my mouth. "You just hush up. We already burned our eyelashes off. You don't have to keep hollerin' at us."

"You what . . . your eyelashes . . . let me see . . . ahhhhug! I never saw anybody without eyelashes before."

"Yeah? How does it look?" Rodney said.

"Well, your eyes are naked, and you look pretty weird. Your eyebrows are all kinked up like a Brill-O pad and . . ."

"Wait'll you see our arms," Jim added.

"You didn't?"

"Yep! Them too!"

"Oh, Momma's going to get you bad!" I said, already heading for the back door. If a sister thinks about it long enough, she can figure out exactly what to say to motivate a mother into action.

I said, "Momma, they've gone and done it! They're ruined for life. Their eyes are naked and their arms too! The hairs . . . they're gone . . . all of them! I told you they—"

That sentence was never finished because Momma did what she does best. She was already out the door, down the steps, and yanking two little boys up by the seat of the pants.

There have been times in my life when I regretted being left out of the scrapes my brothers got into. . . . Their eyelashes grew back longer than mine.

Recalling stories like this one helps me to remember that I was once a child, once a teenager, and also once believed that I knew everything. I remember believing that if my parents would just stick with me, some of my brilliance would rub off on them.

A teenager thinks all parents are born old and that our brains only go back to the age of ancient. Teenagers need to know that we remember being afraid, being lonely, feeling insecure and unsure of ourselves. They need to know that even now we are capable of experiencing those same feelings.

Children want parents who recall being human. I was visiting my three-year-old nephew recently. We were out shopping, and I was pushing him in the shopping cart when suddenly he said, "Aunt Sissie, are you a human bean?"

I said, "Yes, Jarrod, I'm a human bean!"

He thought about it for a minute and said, "Me is a human bean too!"

9

IT ONLY MATTERS
WHEN YOU'RE RELATED
TO THEM
(Embarrassing Moments)

Whenever someone in a family says, "Do we *have* to go?", and they say it as if they're being forced to board the train headed for Siberia, you can be sure it has something to do with the doctor, the dentist, the school, or a recital of one of the other family members.

It's such a joy to get the family ready to attend a recital. They will claim to have never heard of the person having the recital, just to avoid having to go. If you want a vague idea of what a medieval torture chamber sounded like, just listen to the groanings of a family being coerced into dressing for a recital.

This experience is only slightly more enjoyable than smashing your thumb with a ten-pound hammer. Your family will come dragging out to the car like members of a chain gang. Their behavior does so much to bolster the ego of the poor little person having to be *in* the recital. In fact, *they* don't even understand why *they* have to go. You might as well know it now. A recital is something you can make your family attend, but you'll never be able to make them like it.

A recital is a performance given by people who have spent every waking hour for weeks on end trying to memorize something so that they can get up in

149

front of a bunch of people and forget everything they've learned.

A recital is a reality you should consider long and hard when your child says, "Mom, Dad, I would like to study flügelhorn."

First, you should run to the dictionary to see if there really is such an instrument. Then, when you find that there is, you should pause right there to visualize a recital. Say to yourself, "I will be forced to live through the recital. The recital will not be just *any* recital. *The* recital is one that happens in full living technicolor to you and yours—with half the town watching.

Ask yourself, *Do I like living in this town? Do I mind people snickering for years to come when they pass me on the street?* If you can honestly answer no to both of these questions, you are an exceptional person and might consider letting that child study flügelhorn. Or you might just go ahead and let him have the shirt off your back—that would be easier.

No one ever tells a parent what's involved in a recital. When you buy your first piano, it doesn't come with a warning that a recital is lurking somewhere in the background. You just momentarily forget that a recital is where your adorable but imperfectly trained little people will come out in tiny little tuxedos or wearing starched ruffled dresses to perform for the first time in a situation in which it is possible to embarrass every living relative they have.

My mother should have known this because she had humiliated her parents a generation before by walking out to center stage where she proceeded to sing the same phrase of "Somewhere over the Rainbow" twelve times, accompanied only by the hiccups. So how she could have forgotten for one moment the seriousness of a little thing called the recital is a mystery to me.

More Guts Than Talent

My first recital was a long one. I stood in the wings wearing the only red dress I would ever have in my life—I hate red. But it was a cute red dress. It was sheer and went all the way to the floor. It covered my shoes. I could have gotten away with wearing my Red Ball sneakers under there if it hadn't been for Momma. She looked under there, saw my Red Ball sneakers, and took me back home to change.

That night was a night of firsts for me. It was the first time I ever stood in the wings waiting to go on stage. I found out I liked being on stage. All I wanted was for those other people to get off the stage so I could go on. That was the first time I recognized that some people had more guts than talent, and the first time I had ever played a duet in public. It would also be my last time to play a duet in public, in private, or even in my dreams.

Now, listen, I don't want you to think that I thought I was the hottest piano player since Benny Goodman. (My husband just saw this and told me that Benny Goodman never touched a piano in his life, and I said, "Then he was more talented than I realized if he played one without ever touching it." Then my husband informed me that Benny Goodman played clarinet. I said, "I *know* that! It was Jack

Benny who played the piano!" Then my husband left the room with a wild look on his face—so I must be right about it being Jack Benny.)

Anyway, I knew I wasn't more talented than some of those other kids. Some of them had even memorized the exact notes on the sheet music. I preferred to improvise but had failed to notify my music teacher of that detail. I wanted to surprise her.

A duet is something you do with someone else; at least, that's how it works best. I tried playing one by myself once but got a splinter from sliding back and forth on the piano bench.

When the time for my duet arrived, I pranced out on stage and pulled a switch. I decided it would be a lot more interesting if I played my part of the duet on the low end of the piano instead of the high end where I was supposed to be.

My duet partner didn't appreciate the switch. He acted as if he'd never seen the upper half of a piano keyboard before and didn't realize that it contained exactly the same keys, just a lot higher.

That evening put an end to any chances I might have had for a serious piano concert career. In fact, it became obvious to everyone that I was comedy bound. Everyone except my piano teacher, my mother, my daddy, and my duet partner, who didn't like me anymore after that. That piano teacher proved what I had suspected all along: She wouldn't recognize a good joke if she heard it firsthand, which in this case she had—and she didn't.

I also learned that a recital like mine can cause a devoted daddy like mine to say afterward, "That cute little blonde in the red dress? No, I don't believe I know *who* she is."

The Band Concert and the Tin Ear

Our son wanted to study saxophone. Wait a minute—that's not true. He didn't want to *study* it. He wanted to play one without having to study it. In which case he would have been an exceptional talent, and we could have taken him on the road and made a lot of money.

The saxophone was an instrument the child couldn't even pronounce but was sure he could play. All we needed to do was leave him alone with the thing a few days, and he was positive it would just "come" to him. We did consider leaving him alone with it, but he was too young to survive living by himself.

So, we stayed with him and put cotton in our ears for protection. You have to understand: The saxophone is not a nice instrument to put into the wrong hands. You could achieve the same effect by playing a tape of a bull elephant stuck in its mating call.

The day that child learned to make two sounds on the thing, he wanted to run off and audition for the "Late Night with David Letterman" show band. It must take a lot of air to play the saxophone. Our son had as much air as a balloon whizzing around the room and still couldn't quite get the hang of it. He used the reeds for toothpicks and enjoyed showing us how wet he could get them before sticking them on some part of his face.

He mastered loud the first day. We mastered sustained migraines and pained expressions, but neither of us made it past the first band concert.

Let's face it. Playing an instrument isn't for everyone. You have to be able to move your fingers and some part of the brain simultaneously. That's just too much pressure to put on some people.

Our first band concert was a humbling experience. As I've already said, it was also our last band concert. You might say we knew how not to overdo a good thing. We sat close to the back of the room and slouched down in our chairs.

When our son stood up and began to perform, the man next to us leaned over and said, "Do you hear that awful noise?"

We pretended deafness.

He said, "Do they call that playing the saxophone?"

Using my best French accent, I said, "How do jou spell zat?"

He cocked his head and said, "How long have you been here?" I think he meant, "In this country."

I answered, "Too long, too long . . ."

Everybody Takes After Somebody

The person who said "you can't go home again" probably had a mother like mine, and he was intimidated every time he went home.

My mother is strong. She can do anything. I'm not talking about all that stuff that women are "supposed" to be able to do; I'm talking about everything.

She's mechanical and creative. She fixes the plumbing when it's gone awry. She can rewire the kitchen stove. She writes birthday cards that rhyme, and she makes rolls that rise on their own. She's still confused that she has a daughter like me.

I break out in a rash when I pass by anything mechanical. Putting Scotch tape into its dispenser leaves me weak. I am *not* computer friendly, and my own husband had to write out directions for setting my new microwave oven. He ended the directions with "Honey, if you want to wait till I get home, you can." That was the best news I'd had all day. I keep hoping someone will stage a hostile takeover of my kitchen. My husband enrolled me in a remedial cooking class as a birthday gift last year, but I dropped out—the textbook didn't have any pictures.

The person who said you could never go home again must have been raised by the mother who said, "You've made your bed; now you can lie in it." My mother said that to my husband when we got married.

I finally figured out who I take after in my family. One day Momma and I were washing dishes together when we looked out the window and saw Daddy working under the hood of the car. Only half his body was visible. I said, "Look! Daddy must be working on the car."

Momma said, "Yes, and when he gets through with it, we'll have to have it towed to the garage to have it fixed."

Now I know how Momma gave birth to someone who can't *do* anything. . . . I take after my daddy.

These People Can
Really Get Under Your Skin

For some reason we want our relatives to live up to some higher yet unseen measuring stick than the one we expect other people to uphold.

We want them at all times to come across as having "it" all together. My family can rarely figure out exactly what "it" is, much less find it at the same time, then keep it together.

I've been watching people since before I was old enough to know what to call it. My momma used to get onto me about doing it. She'd say, "Sylvia, you quit staring at those people. They'll think there's something wrong with you." Now, why in the world did she care what they thought about me just because I was staring at them? Why wouldn't she say instead, "Stop staring at those people; they might think there's something wrong with *them!*"

She used to think I was a nosy little person; now she thinks I'm a nosy big person.

One of the fascinating things I've noticed about family is that the people related to us have the greatest potential for embarrassing us. We just have a difficult time letting our family be who they are and do things the way they do them.

My husband and I once attended a very nice dinner party in a lovely home. Not long after the meal began, I just happened to notice that one of the wives kept widening her eyes and trying to signal her husband across the table. I couldn't help myself. I stared at her husband, trying to find out what he was doing. He looked perfectly normal to me, but then his wife began to use some kind of sign language I'd never seen before. She was making little gestures with the fingers on her right hand, and her eyes were still bugged out. She looked like she was having a spell or something.

All of a sudden, the husband caught on to her hand signals, picked up his napkin from the table, and put it in his lap. It beat all I've ever seen. Her eyes went back to normal, and she began to eat like the rest of us. Why in the world did she care if he forgot to put his napkin in his lap? Nobody else had noticed it except for me. (And I've already told you how *I* am.)

I've seen incidents similar to this many times and one day finally figured it out. It only matters if you're related to them. We get ourselves in a wad over the mundane so often that we probably don't have any energy left to expend when something really important happens.

The Slurp Heard Around the World

My daddy sometimes slurps his coffee. It matters to Momma. She can be all the way at the other end of the house; if daddy slurps, she'll quit what she's doing to come and stare at him until he figures out what he's done and stops.

That's her job. . . . She's married to Daddy, you see. And because of that I won't have to tell you how much my daddy loves this next story. Daddy tells the story of a country fella' who had a unique way of drinking his coffee. The coffee was always too hot for him, so he would pour a little from his cup into his saucer, blow on it to cool it, then sip it from his saucer. I'll admit, this is a technique you'll never read about in Miss Manners' etiquette book. But one day this family invited the preacher to Sunday lunch. The man's wife gave him specific instructions in no uncertain terms. He was not to pour his coffee into his saucer, nor was he to blow it. . . . In fact, he was not even to *sip* his coffee until after the blessing. She came around with the coffee pot after everyone was seated and filled the cups. No one can tell me exactly how this happened, but the dear man knocked over his coffee cup, spilling all the coffee on the table. He may have been a tad clumsy, but he wasn't at a loss for words.

He said, "Well, Ma, there she goes . . . neither blessed nor blowed."

My dad relates to that man. He just wants to slurp in peace.

Give Me Some
Rose-Colored Glasses, Please!

It's a lot easier to watch other people's children than to watch your own children—particularly if you are in church. If it's someone else's child who is experimenting with thirty-two ways to put a pencil eraser up his nose, you will think it's funny. If it's your own child sitting there with a pencil hanging out of his nose, you'll crawl over eighteen pews of people to snatch that pencil away.

When you hear other parents sharing their griefs about a child's bad report card, you will turn a sympathetic ear and say things like, "It's just part of growing up. It's normal for a child not to want to study," or "They're so brilliant, they're just not challenged."

When it's your own child, you stay up at night crying and wondering if there's any possibility that you came home from the hospital with somebody else's child.

My daddy's an outdoor person. Momma thinks the outdoors is just fine as long as it's been covered in concrete and has wicker chairs sitting all over it.

One day we were all sitting around outside on mother's wicker when Daddy reached down, picked up a handful of dirt, and lifted it to his face. He smelled it, and with a shake of his head he said, "My, my that's great soil . . . nothin' like it."

I watched Momma's face turn the color of a green persimmon. She can't bear the sight of anyone who lives in the same house with her getting that close to dirt or being so fond of it. She's spent most of her life looking for dirt in all the wrong places.

Now, if the next door neighbor had picked up the soil to admire it, Momma would have smiled nicely and would have complimented the man on being an environmentalist or something.

There was a time when I feared I was going to make a career out of embarrassing my family in public. Once I was forced to be the spout on a teapot in my first school play. I was barely old enough to stand on my own, but I was just big enough to be a spout.

When it came time for me to lean over and become the spout, I leaned over too far, too fast, and fell on my head. I stopped the production cold turkey.

The little girl who was the handle on the teapot was one of those perfect little people whose nose was already so far up in the air you couldn't be sure she had one. She said in her best stage voice, "Now what did you do that for?" . . . as if I had planned falling on my head to draw attention away from her.

That night I learned something very important about my parents. They showed me that they were still proud of me. In fact, to hear them tell this story, you'd think I was the highlight of the entire production. That's parental love, and it's been known to bestow self-worth and immense value on a little person growing up.

I have attempted to remember their acceptance of me during the past years. But it was always particularly difficult when I was watching someone related to me in church. Our children could have written the booklet on *A Thousand Ways to Distract Your Parents in Church.* I became so good at sending them "looks" that I earned the nickname "ol' rubber face."

It was always particularly difficult around report card time—and as other disappointments popped up through the years.

All parents have the same difficulty—knowing when to affirm, what to overlook, how to encourage someone who can do better. Learning to accept a family member, flaws and all, and love them just the same.

Yes, it really matters when you're related to them. We want all these people connected with us to look good, to do things "right," to be sharp, so we'll come across as looking good, doing something right, and being sharp. It isn't easy to be proud of someone who is experimenting with a new hair style that looks like a dog with the mange. But God looks into the heart. And that is where the true person lives.

Oh—in case you're wondering when you will ever again have the luxury of paying attention in church instead of watching your children, you will have the luxury of paying attention when your last child goes off to college.

When you no longer have a child in church, you may discover that you've suddenly developed "eye trouble." Your eyes keep wandering over to the spot your child used to occupy, and then you remember that she's not there anymore; then your eyes begin to water, and you need a Kleenex; then you wonder when she'll be coming home again. . . .

This cycle will repeat itself many times, for it is just one in a myriad of symptoms of love.

10

JUST CALL ME HONEY, DARLIN', OR DON'T CALL ME NOTHIN' AT ALL
(Family Nicknames)

My husband was about to walk out the door to go to work. It was a day just about like every other day. I was standing there ready to say goodbye when he kissed me and said, "I'll see you this evening; have a good day, princess." Well, ten minutes later, he was long gone, but I was still standing at the back door with my mouth open.

The minute he called me "princess," I realized that I'd forgotten to put on my tiara that morning. I was afraid the man had gone completely mad or blind—or maybe he really loves me! I was standing there wearing no makeup, my hair looked like it had just lived through a tornado, and I was wearing the sweat pants with a hole in them. How in the world can a man say goodbye to something looking like that, call it "princess," and still come home at night. It must be love!

There's something touching about a six-foot man calling his wife "princess." He also likes to call me "baby cakes." I've never asked him whether I'm a cinnamon roll or a honey bun, but this one makes me feel as if I should be smeared with butter and placed beside a hot cup of coffee. Then he would have three of his favorite things together.

Like most of you, we have a list of little endearments we call each other. There's a hidden language that families use. It's a type of underground love language that most of us take for granted and might be embarrassed for the rest of the world to know about. This hidden language is another one of the threads running through families.

Love just seems to bring out the softy in us. No one can say when this tradition begins; you just wake up one morning calling your wife a new name. And without even thinking about it, she answers to it.

At this point, you're sitting there grinning from ear to ear, remembering the pet names you have in your family.

Many of us may use the same nicknames, but no one seems to mind if we borrow from each other. The endearment *honey* tops the list of old standards. It seems as if everyone has borrowed this endearment, and no one seems bothered by the fact that there are probably 189 million honeys in America alone. Why, you add up all the honeys in England, France, Australia and there's no telling what the final count would be. It doesn't matter, when you call your husband or wife "honey," they know you're talking to them and to no one else. They know they're special.

The only time this word isn't special is when a waitress says, "Can I take your order, honey?" When this happens, you are probably on vacation somewhere in Tennessee, Mississippi, Alabama, Texas, or even Missouri. When a waitress uses this word, it doesn't mean she loves you. It means she's being especially friendly and deserves a good tip. Now, if she calls you honey, but forgets what you ordered, she's blown her tip no matter what she calls you.

The South may have a unique collection of terms of endearment. Some of these may bring a blush to your cheeks. There are dumplin', baby cakes, sweets, cutie pie, snookums, sugarplum, and shug, which is short for sugar (that's what you call a nickname within a term of endearment). There are punkin', puddin', baby doll, sweetheart, and of course, as already mentioned, honey! These names could make you hungry just thinking about them.

Pass the Butter, Your Royal Highness, Honey

While the word *honey* is used the world over, it may have limited use in some circles. I tried to picture Prince Philip calling Queen Elizabeth "honey." I pictured him saying, "Your Royal Honey," and it just didn't seem right. In fact, just the thought of it made me laugh out loud. And I bet that Princess Diana is sick of being called "princess." She would probably love to have someone call her "cutie pie."

Although this practice of using "terms of endearment" is universal, different parts of the world have their own unique languages. In America alone, the North and South are different. The North and South have called each other a few names in the distant past, but none of them was a term of endearment.

Those of you in the North do have your own way of talking and your own customs within the family. For instance, you would never be comfortable using the term *darlin'*. If you were to slip and say this to someone in the privacy of your home, you would go into another room and smack yourself. One reason for this is that you talk faster than the rest of us, and using the word *darlin'* just takes too much time. So the word for darlin' in the North would be *hey, you.*

I met one particular woman from the North who said, "You women in the South know two words—*cute* and *darlin'."* I didn't think this was very cute because when she said this I had just called her "darlin'."

If you live in the North, you will select a special name for someone. A family member who grows a beard might be affectionately called Fuzzy. This could get pretty interesting if someone else in the same family grows a beard. You could have Fuzzy and Wuzzy living under the same roof. Nicknames like this are wonderful for the little nieces and nephews who for the first years of their lives don't speak clearly anyway. They will have it made. Uncle Fuzzy is a lot easier to say than Uncle Theodore.

Nieces and nephews are very creative in conferring nicknames on other family members. I have an Aunt Julia who had her name permanently changed by the first niece born to our family. That niece called her JuJu, and that's why she's called JuJu to this very day.

If you grow up to be a very tall person and live in the North, your family would probably call you Shorty. If you're a natural-born track and field star and live above the Mason-Dixon line, your family will probably call you Legs or Speedy. It's easy to see how this sets a person apart in his or her own little niche in life.

All of us may be more alike than we realize. Some of these differences have crossed the Mason-

Dixon line in both directions. My mother was as southern as Scarlett O'Hara, but her daddy called her Midget. Right away you know what that says about my mother. She was very small. To this day she has a measure of pride in her voice when she says, "And my papa always called me Midget."

The terms *sugarplum, sweets, puddin'*, and *dumplin'* are in a category of their own. I'm beginning to believe that somewhere along the way we've confused food and the people we love. This doesn't surprise me because more often than not the two go together in our family.

The day anyone in our family gets together for more than three minutes without someone bringing up the subject of food will be the day after we find out that Brussels sprouts are the only things left in the entire world to eat.

My brother calls me cutie, he calls my sister cutie, and I think I heard him call his beagle dog cutie.

I am thankful my husband doesn't call me puddin'. Both of us are easily swayed by the power of suggestion. Every time he called me puddin', I'd head for the refrigerator and in no time at all my body would assume the appearance of a duffel bag full of basketballs. Then before long my nickname would have to be Pudgy, and then I'd be in a bad mood, so he'd have to call me Stormy. He still calls me baby cakes once in a while, and I finally realized why I buy those miniature pastries and hide them under my pillow.

Most of the time, he calls me darlin', and we probably sound like a couple of hard-core, half-crazed southern lovebirds. I asked him why he occasionally slips and calls me princess? He said it's easier than trying to remember my name.

So much for feeling like royalty.

My Wife's Name Is Ethel

Chances are, if you happen to be from a family that does not have private little names for each other, you may not understand any of this. You are probably sitting there saying to yourself, "My wife's name is Ethel, so I call her Ethel;" or "My husband's name is Barnard, and that's what I call him." That's just fine.

On the surface it makes sense to call them what their names are. It may even appear silly or beneath your dignity to call them anything else. Some of you men would rather take your in-laws on vacation in a Yugo with no air conditioning than be caught calling your wife baby cakes.

But consider this: I am fairly confident that if all the husbands, wives, and children in the world were lined up, if they were blindfolded and could only use one word to call to pick their precious persons out of a crowd, my husband and I could find each other. There might be several thousand Sylvias, but there'd be only two or three princesses. And it wouldn't take him long to narrow it down to me.

We even have nicknames for the children. When my husband calls the youngest boy Wee Willy, you can be sure the boy has an instant reaction. He quickly looks around to see if all the windows are down, then he says, "Is anybody else here?" If the answer is no, then he might answer his daddy.

A private nickname is also a safety precaution. A perfect example of this happened at a baseball game when this same child was just a little tyke. He became separated from us in the crowd. We did what every other calm, in-control set of parents would do . . . we panicked. We began yelling his given name at the top of our lungs. In two minutes flat, there were twelve little boys standing around us who all had the same first name, but none of them looked like the one we had lost.

"This isn't working," I said.

"No kidding!"

So we pulled out all the stops and began yelling, "Wee Willy—Wee Willy!"

When we did that, two things happened instantly. All those other boys knew they didn't belong to us, and our own Wee Willy came crawling out from under a bleacher with a grin on his face. We might never have found him if he hadn't had a nickname.

The boy's a bit older these days, and we use that nickname sparingly—mainly when we want to be sure he's paying attention.

A term of endearment can make someone feel very special, set apart from all the other people in the world. When my husband slips and calls me Sylvia, I think he's upset about something.

I can't really say what all of this means or how this came into existence, but I know what it *doesn't* mean. It doesn't mean that we're odd, crazy, or neurologically inferior as one magazine article on this subject tried to imply.

All it means is that we love each other, and we'd be able to find each other if we got lost at a baseball game.

Even Security Has a Thousand Names

The first time I laid eyes on my husband's three boys, the youngest one was clutching something unidentifiable to his breast.

"What's that?" I asked under my breath.

"That? Oh, that's his *B*," he said, as if it were perfectly normal to have a death grip on something dark brown that looked as if it had been used to clean up an oil spill in the Atlantic.

"Hmm . . . *B* . . . is that short for 'bacteria' or what?"

"*B*" my husband responded as if I'd never heard of children.

"*B* as in blanket . . . you know, the soft, fuzzy things you get at baby showers before you're born and go to sleep with every night for years to come."

This child was not only born owning this thing, he looked as if he had every intention of going off to college with it. He refused to let anyone wash it, and he went into fits if he became separated from it.

When at age eight he finally informed us we could launder the nasty thing, his father picked up all three threads and placed them on a piece of electrician's tape and soaked them for two days in the sink. The threads of the big *B* are still stuck to the electrician's tape hanging on a bulletin board in this nearly grown person's room. And I promise you that now and then I catch him rubbing against it with a smile on his face.

The daughter of one of our friends creatively named her blanket her "meme." We know another family who called their grandmother "Meme," but they never clutched her to their breast while sucking a thumb, and being around her never made them want to curl up in a ball and go to sleep.

My sister's security as a child was to rub the satin edge on her blanket; she called it her "wanket." She would fix that satin in her fingers, take a few rubs off it, and fall fast asleep. She admits to this day being overly fond of satin comforters and the edges on blankets. So you have to wonder . . . Do we ever get over the attachment to the "wanket" or our "meme"?

I don't know what came first—the need for security, the blanket, or a grandmother, but all of them are important and will answer to just about any name.

I didn't have a *B* or a "meme" when I was a little girl. My husband says that's why I do funny things with the edge on my pillow case after I'm asleep. . . . He may be right.

Let's Just Call It Hot

I don't actually remember what my brother Jim called me the day I rubbed red pepper all over his face pretending it was makeup. He was only six, but don't let that fool you. A six-year-old boy with red-hot pepper on his lips and cheeks can make a nine-year-old sister feel she's just done the unpardonable. I love my brother. I loved my brother even then. To this day, when this subject comes up, he says, "If you loved me, why did you rub red-hot pepper all over me?"

I wish I knew. Because if I knew why, then I'd tell him, and we would both have some sort of reason. I thought the red color of the red pepper would rub

off on his face and he'd be cute with red lips. It did—
he wasn't.

Not only was he not cute, he wasn't happy. Then
my parents weren't happy. Then I wasn't happy. The
next thing I knew, we were the unhappiest bunch of
people you've ever seen or heard. My brother was
crying and rubbing his face. I started crying because
he was crying—and started rubbing my face with the
same hands I had used to rub pepper all over his
face. Then my face looked just like his face—and I
was crying for the same reason he was crying. We
were both crying because we were on fire. The tears
fell on our cheeks, and I learned that salty water on
red-hot peppered skin is like fuel on a flame. The
crying rose to squalling, alternated with bellowing,
and then went back to squalling again.

We were visiting our paternal grandparents when
this little episode began. Actually, we were in the
back seat of the car on the way home from Granny's
when I discovered that red pepper in the brown
paper bag in the floorboard. All my life the worst
things have happened to me in the car, and this was
probably the beginning.

My daddy turned that car around on three cents
and presto! We were zooming down Bradyville Pike
in the opposite direction. We screeched into the
driveway at Granny's, and for once no one was expecting us. Daddy yanked our squalling bodies into
the house and presented us to Granny, hoping for
some miracle cure.

When Granny died, she was still telling this story.
That sounds like she died *from* telling it. What I mean
is, many years later, when Granny died, she still

loved to tell this story and have a good laugh about it. She'd be pleased to know that this little incident has not been allowed to die a natural death.

What Granny did was to laugh out loud while she rubbed Pond's cold cream and some kind of lard all over our faces. The cold cream smelled nice and made us look weird but did nothing to put out the fire. We looked like two greased, red-faced little pigs going back out to the car that day.

It was late, late—make that very late—in the day before I was happy again. My brother didn't want me to be happy for a long time after that.

When we would be downtown with Mother and she would stop to talk to friends or be trying to purchase something, my brother would butt right in to the middle of the conversation. He'd point to me and say, "She did it to me!"

Then, when they politely ignored him, he would say, "She set fire to my little face in the back seat of my daddy's car!" He said it like I was an arsonist with a thing for little boys' faces.

Momma did a lot of explaining for the rest of that year, and I paid dearly for what is now called the "Red Pepper Episode" of my life.

I'm not fond of red peppers to this day, and my brother Jim likes them almost as much as I do.

As I said when I began this story, I don't remember what he called me that day, but based on what I do recall from growing up with my particular parents, he probably didn't call me anything and get away with it. You have to understand that we were not even permitted to use the words *stupid* or *dumb* when referring to another human being. The same

rule applied to siblings even though there were times
we didn't believe them to be human.

Even now, when I refer to a "thing" as stupid, my
mother's face flashes before my mind's eye, and I
have an uncontrollable urge to ask forgiveness.

I'm sure that in the process of growing up there
were numerous times that one of us did something
which by definition qualified for stupid, ignorant, or
dumb, but make no mistake, nobody—nobody—was
permitted to identify it as such to our faces, behind
our backs, or under their breath.

This may seem pretty strange in a world where
name calling has become a secondary career. I've had
it up to the last pore on my forehead with people
getting laughs by exercising their vocabulary calling
people insulting names. This ol' world needs a hearty
dose of my mother.

This practice of not calling anyone stupid is one that
my husband and I have tried to pass on to our boys.

Years ago one of our sons put a firecracker in a
fruit jar and lit it while holding it in his hand. When
my husband returned from the emergency room
where a doctor had tediously removed all the glass
from this boy's body, I had a moment of hysteria.

"That was a stupid thing to do!" I said.

"Dad, she called me stupid!" the boy said.

"No son. She said *that* was a stupid thing to do,
and I'm inclined to agree with her!"

"Then *you're* calling me stupid," the boy insisted.

After a brief pause, my husband said, "Let me put
it this way, son: Putting a firecracker in a glass jar and
lighting it comes pretty close to qualifying you for stu-

pid, but it definitely doesn't give you credit for using all the brilliance which I passed on to you."

That seemed to settle it, and the word *stupid* never came up again. That boy is now a successful adult, probably because nobody called him stupid even when he deserved it.

I guess I can thank my momma for teaching me the importance of the words we use with each other—so that years later when I had a family of my own I would understand the significance of good communication.

11

IT MUST HAVE BEEN SOMETHING I SAID
(Communication)

Did you know that after you had children you would never be allowed to finish a sentence again? We know a woman who talks in half sentences. My husband thinks she has a learning disability, but I understand her perfectly. She has children.

Communicating is never the same after children come along. This is when a couple discovers that communication in the family requires more skill than snow skiing and more time than an eight-day clock. Communicating even requires us to pay attention, which means to listen with acute interest, no matter how many times we've heard it before.

Time and attention are two of the most valuable commodities a family can give each other. They are expensive gifts because when you give someone else your time, you give up part of yourself. Before I married, I searched for years trying to find someone who wanted my heart. Now it seems as if people are standing in line to relieve me of parts I'm not ready to give up. But mostly everyone in my family seems to need the same parts—my time and my undivided attention.

Children require time and attention from their parents and will go to great lengths to get *some* attention even if it's the wrong variety or from other people. The place where they really need attention is at home.

If you want your children to listen to you, pretend you're talking on the telephone. It doesn't matter where they are or what they're doing, you get on the phone and they'll appear out of nowhere. They think it is their temporary calling in life to talk to you while you're on the phone.

It's truths like this that cause a mother and father to begin the habit of tuning out those everyday interruptions. This is a dangerous habit—tuning out the small everyday moments—because one day something important will happen when you're not looking.

Life moves on whether or not you're paying attention, and there are no instant replays. You can blink your eyes, and those little ones drooling on your shoulder will be begging for the keys to the car. Or they will inform you that while you turned your head, they had their first date.

What it really says to our children when we pay attention is that we're interested in them. And if you can honestly convey that fact, children will open up and communicate more. You might even avoid hiring the CIA to figure out what they're up to later on.

The key word is *listen*. Especially if you have an adolescent person under your roof. One word from a teenager is water on parched ground, and you, the parent, are the parched ground. You want them to talk, need them to talk to you.

Children have a natural ability which rarely gets appreciated. They can tell you something that you need to know without telling you everything you need to know. They are so good at it that often they'll tell you something without telling you *anything!*

This is why mothers become great detectives. They have to be good at reading between the lines. Reading between the lines will eventually lead them to what a child *really* means.

This is usually the mother's job because, for some reason, fathers will fall for just about anything.

One of my friends told her husband that something was troubling their daughter. So he went upstairs to check on her as any loving father should do. When he came down a few minutes later, my friend said, "Well, did you find out what's wrong with her?"

He said, "There's nothing wrong with her."

She asked him how he figured that out, and he said, "Because I asked her if anything was wrong, and she said she was 'just fine,' so she's fine."

This is only one of many areas in which mothers and fathers need each other. A father can be too pragmatic, and a mother can be too analytical—not often, but it is possible.

It's a mother's job to figure out what's wrong and let the father in on it. It would be very helpful if children and spouses arrived with a handbook listing the true meanings of all the statements they'll make in an average lifetime that someone else will have to sit up late at night trying to figure out.

What It Means When . . .

It will help children to open up and talk if you have already established good listening skills before you have a crisis. When your thirteen-year-old daughter takes a flying leap into adolescence and refuses to talk while she's figuring out whatever it is she's supposed to do as a teenager, even the sound of silence can speak volumes, and someone should be listening. When she finally emerges from her room and breaks her code of silence, be prepared to hear every word and pick up on every little nuance. She will most likely be speaking a language you've never heard and can't come close to understanding, but good eye contact can make up for a world of ignorance on your part.

When your teenager begins to come home and says things like, "Dad, I'm having a 'little' trouble in math," you need to know that what she really means is, "Dad, I have failed math, and it's already too late for you to do anything about it."

Teenagers are sensitive people, and where they get it is a mystery to me. It couldn't be in the genes because sometimes a parent has all the sensitivity of a piece of sandpaper.

For instance, if your sixteen-year-old has just had the first major heartbreak of her life after having only two dates, Dad will come home, notice her swollen eyes, and blurt out, "What's the matter? Did you and Ryan break up already?" That goes over like a lead balloon, and the howling sound leaving the room faster than the speed of light will be your daughter. It can take days to clean up a mess like that.

Our family developed a perfect solution for this sort of crisis. I had some cue cards printed up to flash the second anyone walks in the door. The children can even be trained to use them. We have a card that says, "Shaky Ground," which means "tread gently and speak slowly. Someone's already in a touchy mood—don't make it worse!" We have another sign which reads, "Celebration." This cues us that something wonderful has happened and needs to be noticed, like a seventy instead of a thirty-eight on a physiology exam. The sign that says, "Gloom 'n' Doom," means just the opposite of "Celebration."

The sign "Pitiful Pearl is Here" means that someone is wearing feelings like very fragile shoulder pads, so touch at your own risk, or you could draw back a nub.

If we come home and there's a sign on the refrigerator that says, "Hi Mom and Dad, everything's fine!" we call the school's guidance counselor immediately. This means the child is walking blissfully into la-la land and not at all bothered by never turning in homework.

When your senior in high school comes home and says, "I need some note cards, Mom," go ahead and run away from home. It means "I have a fifty-page senior term paper due day after tomorrow and haven't written the first word." This is one of those times when you wish you could just hire someone to pay attention to this family for you, so you could sleep at night.

It's a Dog's Job

The term paper is a favorite cause of nightmares in our house. Our youngest son was originally exposed to the term paper in the sixth grade, but it didn't take. He informed me at two o'clock the day before this notorious paper was due. I listened to him; then I cried. Then I took him to the public library and left him. Seven hours of writing later he was still at the library. When no one else had claimed him and he had a term paper, we picked him up.

The seven-hour paper consisted of an introduction. The subject was dogs. At first glance I thought the child was brilliant, that he had actually pulled it off at the ninth hour. Then I proceeded to read six and a half pages of dog names. That masterpiece took seven and a half hours of hard labor—more time than it takes for most children to be born!

Listen Now! Later Doesn't Count

There are numerous statements that a child will make, and you'd better be paying attention at the time because later will be too late. An example of this happened in our family as we were driving down the beautiful Blue Ridge Parkway. "I don't feel too good," the child said feebly from the back seat. You need to understand that this little person had developed a pretty good career in not feeling too good for absolutely no reason at all, so I continued to enjoy the scenery and waited for his second clue. The second clue never came. So when a child says, "I'm not feeling too good," there are two approaches. If you are at home, first you look closely at them. If they look even halfway normal simply walk them into the bathroom and help them sit down. They immediately feel better, and most of them do not want to be sick anywhere near the bathroom—that would be too easy.

Now, if you are in the car when your child says he's not feeling too good, *pull over immediately!* Don't waste time looking at him. You can rest assured he looks something like the color of Swiss cheese that's been around too long. In fact, *if* you can be so sharp as to anticipate all this before the child says a word, you might be able to get off the road in time.

When our son said, "I'm not feeling too good," for the second time, my husband yanked the car off the road. The child opened his door, leaned over, and threw up in the back seat.

This child has a gag reflex that should be studied by medical science. He can smile and throw up in eighteen directions simultaneously, then turn around and feel like a million dollars ready to go while the rest of us are making tracks getting away from the scene. For several years I didn't take him anywhere without an airline "sick sack" clipped to his shirt.

In contrast to this kind of child is the toddler who refuses to let you know there's anything wrong. When your toddler is standing in front of you with his semi-toothless grin on his face and Old Faithful running down his legs into his first pair of miniature Nikes and onto your tile floor, you will ask what may be the least intelligent question in all of motherhood: "Darlin', do you need to go to the bathroom?"

"Uh-huh!" he will say emphatically, shaking his head back and forth for no to be sure you get it.

A good rule of thumb is that by the time you suspect that he needs to do something, he's already done it.

These kinds of experiences are the parents' testing ground just to be sure we are paying attention. By the time a mother and dad survive one or more children and all the various stages of growing up, they're so accustomed to guessing games like Name-the-Cause-with-Barely-a-Clue, that winning on "Wheel of Fortune" would be second nature. It's no wonder that show is so popular.

Sometimes a child will say something that needs no interpretation. Once I was comforting a neighbor's little girl who was crying. I said, "Don't you know it makes you homely to cry so much?"

She quit crying and said, "You musta cried a lot when you was little." I knew exactly what she meant.

When your teenager says, "Dad, I'll be needing a 'little' more money before school is out this year," it means he has lost most of his books and won't be getting a report card until you pay for them.

When your son says, "I had a little accident today," it means he has ripped a hole the size of a football in the new thirty-eight-dollar slacks you begged him not to wear to school.

When your twelve-year-old calls you at work with newfound knowledge like, "Did you know liquid Joy is amazing stuff?" it means he has put a bottle of that amazing stuff in your dishwasher for the fun of it, and you need to call "Suds-on-Wheels" to have your house suctioned out.

A Turned Back Is Not Your Best Side

There is not a man, woman, or child who does not desire to be noticed. We desire those people around us to be available at least some of the time and to express loving concern when we come to them. The

heavenly Father is available to us at a moment's notice. What if we went to Him with our cares, our
hearts' desires, and heard the words, "Not now, child
. . . in a minute, son. . . . Can't you see I'm busy?
Come back later."

What kind of Father would He be?

Failure to pay attention at frequent intervals
might force you to take drastic measures, like plastic
surgery to have an extra set of eyeballs installed in
the back of your head. The portable phone was invented by a mother who turned her back one time
too many.

It's so very easy to do. I know a young mother
who turned her back a little too long. When she
found her children, she also found that the dirt from
her ficus tree had left its pot and was resting peace-
fully on her new peach carpet. The dirt had been
turned into a country lane with cars and trucks going
down it. A day like this will be the day your vacuum
cleaner malpractices and refuses to take in foreign
particles.

You don't have to be a Rhodes scholar to understand how important paying attention can be. But
just how long can you pay attention before your
brain begins to sizzle from overuse?

I am personally acquainted with some committed,
dedicated parents. They try to remain alert at all
times. They don't look like it most of the time but
they try. Let's be honest: Rearing children gives you
a graduate degree in listening to tedium. And you
can only take so much tedium before your eyes begin
to walk in circles.

Some of you have children like ours; they are the masters of details. We have one who is particularly good with important details, like the blow-by-blow account of every movie he sees. He gives you the dialogue, the costume changes, and angles of all the cameras, then lets you know which actors had dirt under their fingernails. This is the same child who can't remember to flush, brush, make up, pick up, or find anything that belongs to him. He can't remember if he has homework and forgets to close the refrigerator door. This was the child who began a story when he was in sixth grade and finished it the night he graduated from eighth grade.

I said to him once, "Son, do you have homework?"

"Not really," he said. Then pausing to consider his options, he said, "Well, I do have a 'little' quiz in physiology."

I asked him if a little quiz in physiology was like someone being a little bit pregnant, and he never answered me.

We already knew that a little quiz in physiology was a *big* deal because parts of the body did not come naturally to this boy.

He told us that if God had wanted us to understand the duodenum, He should have hung it on the outside of our bodies like ears, so we could see it. It is obvious that the boy has never seen the duodenum and has no idea how ugly it is and how awful it would look hanging on the side of his head.

Amazing! And this was the same young man standing before us telling us more than we ever dared to ask about a movie we never wanted to see. I sat there slapping my cheeks to stay alert until the end, nodding occasionally to prove I was right there with him. Then I tore my eyes away to smile at my husband and discovered he had developed "Novocaine brain" and was taking a nap with his eyes wide open.

I poked him in the side, and he came back to earth with a jolt.

"Ah . . . yes . . . son," he said. "Very interesting. Now where were we?"

That child put his brain in *B* for Backup and started at the beginning.

Sometimes this can be so boring that flies quit moving around in the room.

"Excuse me, I think the phone is about to ring!" I said as I left the room.

This should tell you how important it is to pay attention the first time!

What I Think You Said Is Not What You Thought I Heard or Something Like That

Sometimes life seems like one gigantic fill-in-the-blanks workbook. Some of us spend our lives making all the blanks, and others fill them in. I have always been a big fan of the direct approach. But for some reason, life is lived on a mound of understatement and innuendo. It is my belief that life would get a lot easier if someone could take all the guesswork out of it. (But it would also become tediously boring.)

Husbands and wives even have to pay attention to each other. Sometimes *we* don't say exactly what we mean either.

If your wife calls you at work to mention casually that she "had a little trouble with the garage door today," you need to know what she really means. She means she forgot to use the garage door opener today—which means you no longer have a garage door and no longer need an opener.

When your daughter who is a college freshman decides to bring a "friend" home for the first time and says, "There's a little something you should know about Harve," it means that it could be a very long weekend because Harve has three pigtails (two blond, one natural) and lives on powdered milk and sesame seeds.

When you ask your college daughter how she's doing in school, if she says, "It's very enlightening," it means she's discovered that she can no longer pull a solid *B* without cracking a book the way she did in high school. When this happens, you—the parent—will very soon be enlightened too.

When your neighbor leaves a message on your phone answering device which says, "We need to talk about your dog," it means that your dog has skillfully managed to relocate the neighbor's flower bed from the front yard to the back. And you are responsible for replacing three thousand dollars worth of landscaping—that or move in the middle of the night.

When your in-laws call in the middle of the night and say, "We've had the most delightful idea," it means they had the idea of coming for a surprise visit and are already at a pay phone six blocks from your house.

When your husband comes home from work with a weird look on his face and says, "It's been a *most* unusual day today!" what he means is that he accidentally faxed his necktie to Milwaukee.

If he says he had a "little trouble at work," it means his secretary had a PMS attack, locked herself in the file room, and forged a purchase order for a boxcar load of Hershey Kisses!

If your husband calls you from work and says, "Brace yourself, Harriett," what he means is, "Start packing. You've been transferred for the twenty-eighth time!"

When your young adult daughter is settled in her first apartment after college and calls you to say, "We have the most wonderful apartment. . . . It has a view," she doesn't mean she is overlooking nature. She means she has a clear view of the swimming pool and wants a pair of binoculars for her birthday.

Listening is a lifetime commitment and is followed closely by paying attention. Neither one is worth a plugged nickel without the other.

Another truth from all this is that anytime anybody related to you says he thinks he's getting a "little" something, take him seriously. You can carve this in stone and put it on your bathroom mirror: When the word *little* is used, call the Red Cross disaster relief immediately.

When the word *little* comes out of the mouth of an adolescent, prepare for a crisis somewhere on the scale of the destruction of Atlanta in *Gone with the Wind*.

In our family, not only do we sometimes fail to understand what we hear; we understand even less of what we read. We took up writing notes to each other as schedules became more and more complicated. We even had rules for writing notes: what to write them on and where to leave them. I've saved most of the notes from our youngest son. Someday in my old age I plan to get them out, consult a language expert, and try to decipher them. It should keep me busy for years.

If you think children have an interesting way of expressing themselves verbally, they become even more interesting when they put words on paper.

Wouldn't you love finding this note on your chopping block in the kitchen: "Mom, I dropped something of yours today, but it must not have been a good one cause it went all to pieces when it first hit the floor. I'm sorry, but you should buy better stuff!"

My husband was just crazy over this one: "Dad, somebody called and asked me to tell you something, but I forgot what it was. He said you would know him. I forgot his name. Love, Your Son. P.S. At least I did remember to leave you a note that he called."

I was just wild about this note; in fact, it may be my favorite of all the notes saved over the last several years. We have a family rule that even if you have your own wheels, you have to let someone know where you're going, when you'll return, and other "vitals."

The note said: "Mom, I was here when I wrote this, but I'm not now. If I'm still not here when you get home, let me know cause I'll be at John's."

It All Started with the Parkay

Something vital began to slip away from us when the television was permitted to become a member of the family. We began to confuse sitting around together with communicating with each other. That's the trouble with television. Somebody is always watching one when there is something more important that they should be doing, like using their God-given minds to communicate with other members of the family. We decided to do something about it. We put our family on a limited television viewing schedule. We are only allowed to watch five commercials per week.

A television commercial is powerful. A commercial could persuade an eighty-year-old great-great-grandmother to reenlist in motherhood for a second go 'round.

The effect on our family has reached an all time high. Even my mother believes every commercial she sees. She honestly believes that every coffee bean that comes out of South America is personally hand-picked by someone named Juan Valdez.

She watched one Geraldo Rivera show and is ruined for life. If she sees three little old ladies standing together outside a coffee shop, she thinks they're a gang, and anyone with dark-tinted windows in his car is a drug dealer.

And to this day my daddy believes that a city is a terrible place you go when you're ready to lose all your American Express checks.

Not only does television affect our thinking, but it takes irreplaceable time from us.

One of our sons has always believed everything he hears on television. He used to know every commercial and do all the voices, so nobody has to convince me of the effect of television on the family. Once this child wanted to hide in the refrigerator to catch the Parkay talking. We had a tough time convincing him that Parkay is only permitted to talk on television.

Sometimes I go to McDonald's to watch people. I watch families on the playground, and it can be a most revealing experience.

You can tell which parents are really into their children and which ones are not. To some mothers, the playground is a thank-goodness-they're-off-my-hands-for-a-while place.

Other parents remain totally involved with their children, watching as the child comes down the slide, applauding, laughing, or simply smiling—being involved.

Some parents have a love in their faces that communicates to the child: I'm here; I'm with you, ever watching.

All the children desire to be watched. I can tell as they glance up occasionally and check on the parent, waiting to be noticed.

They glance up eagerly looking for that certain smile of affirmation, for that look from a parent that has the power to build self-worth in a little person. A look from an interested parent can say, "You're something special to me;" "You're worth noticing;" and "I'm here for you."

This experience caused me to wonder how many children will grow into adulthood still searching for someone to *really* notice them. How many will try everything imaginable just to locate that important something to give them the self-worth never granted in childhood?

There are mothers and dads who will receive a special blessing in heaven simply because they took time to pay attention.

The greatest hoax perpetrated on the modern family may be the myth of "quality time." The only true quality time is "plenty of time." The myth of quality time is always espoused by a parent who never gives enough time.

If children truly spell love *t-i-m-e,* there are some adults who need to learn to spell again.

When You Are Tempted

Finally, when you are tempted to be too busy to pay attention, that in itself is a pretty good clue that you'd better do it anyway.

One day as I was just beginning to recover from cleaning up a dozen eggs off the kitchen floor, a voice called from another room, "Mom, the dog's making a funny noise!"

"Well, laugh at her!" I said.

"Mom, It's not *that* kind of funny."

Later when I was cleaning up the funny noise the dog had been making, I couldn't help thinking how much more fun it would have been to have paid attention the first time.

12

FACTS, FICTION, AND MYTHS
(Finding the Truth Somewhere)

Somewhere back in time, somebody makes a rash statement, and someone else overhears it and repeats it. Then you have the law of gossip coming into effect: Anything that is repeated three times becomes the truth. That's how a myth begins.

Somewhere back in time a man was overheard talking in a restaurant. He said, "Your marriage will get better *after* children." Everyone sitting near the man heard the statement and went home to set about the task of proving it.

I believe this saying was actually spoken for the first time by a man whose last child had just left home. In this case, the statement ceases to be a myth and stands a very good possibility of being true—especially if the marriage was solid in the beginning.

A marriage needs a sturdy foundation *before* children enter the picture. Children don't come into the world for the express purpose of granting stability to a relationship. The only stability they've ever known is left behind at birth. They expect to find more of the same in their new world, but they are not allowed to bring any with them. How much stability would you have if all you could do is cry, spit, burp, and sleep in one-hour intervals? How secure would you feel if you couldn't even focus your eyes. And how would you like it if people got down in your face and blubbered in some kind of foreign language: "Oh, boo, boo, goo, goo, Ma-Ma's ba-be . . . oooy, oou, sooo fweet."

A baby is a package of love wrapped up in tiny little skin. A baby is a bundle of mystery that makes squeaky noises and smells funny. A baby is a living wake-up call. A baby is a miniature mind waiting to be filled. A baby is the biggest change that will ever come over a couple in their entire lives together. A baby is the square root of love. You need love to bring one into your life, you need even more love to rear one, and you need an even larger dose of love when it's time to let them go.

We have these mysterious neighbors who live three doors down the street. We've never met them. We've never seen them. They are rarely at home. Their yard is always neat. The house is nearly always dark inside. They drive nice cars. They have an automatic outdoor light, which our dog sets off every night when we go for a walk. Their yard is pretty, and flowers are always growing in the planters out front during summer.

I tell you I have just about gone crazy with curiosity.

Then one evening we walked past the house, and hanging from the front door was the largest pink bow since the opening of the shopping mall. Both the cars were in the driveway plus a few extras. And standing in the front yard was a stork, announcing, "Baptist Hospital delivers." It was a girl—and that house hasn't been the same since. The daddy's car didn't leave the driveway for three weeks straight.

All the lights are on just about any time of the day or night, and the mother doesn't work anymore. They bought a new vehicle, sturdier than the cute little sports thing the mother drove before. It came with a child's car seat already installed in the back seat, and 4-wheel drive. She hasn't been anywhere in it yet. It just sits there ready to go. She's already heard about carpooling, and she's prepared.

We passed by the other night, and the father was out watering his grass. I said, "How's your baby?"

He grinned and said, "She's incredible! She's great! In fact, I'm listening to her right now!" And he held up the nursery monitor in his right hand like a brick of gold. I liked him right away. He's changed more than his schedule since that little girl came into his life. And that's only the beginning of all the changes that he'll be required to make in one life-time. Their life is no longer a mystery to me. I know "exactly" what they're doing at just about any given moment.

A marriage needs a sturdy foundation before children enter the picture, and it needs a sturdy one when they come onto the scene. And it should be a solid rock when there are no more children left at home.

Myth: You Can Forget Where You Came From

It's never my intention to eavesdrop. You can blame it on restaurants that place tables too close together. That, and the fact that I was just sitting in this restaurant one day with my ears hanging out when all of a sudden this woman started to cry out loud, and I started to listen. (That, and my husband says I'm nosy too.)

"He's just a baby . . . only twenty . . . and he's . . . dropped out of college." (sob) "Said he had to go 'find' himself!" (She spat out the word *find* with enough vehemence to rattle dishes.)

"He said he wanted to use his college money to finance the search for his missing self."

That's when I thought, *She's just crying because they gave him the money!*

Her friend was listening, trying to be sympathetic. She said, "I don't blame you for being upset. Why, that's just awful that he's dropped out of school."

At this point the crying woman said, "No, I'm upset because we gave all that money to somebody who doesn't even know who he is!"

All your life you hear about adult children like this, and you never understand it. You look at other people and wonder how they could be so normal and manage to rear a child like that.

Then you become the proud parent of one yourself and find that you understand it even less than you suspected.

When your own twenty-year-old comes home and drops the bomb—he doesn't know "who" he is or "where" he is in life, and he doesn't know "why." If you have one of these children and are wondering what he will grow up to be, you can eliminate the field of journalism. They have a definite problem with the five "W's"—the who, what, when, where, and especially the why.

When one of our sons told us he didn't know for sure who he was and needed to find himself, we walked him into the bathroom and told him to take a good long look around. He'd spent the better part of his life in that little room, so if he had misplaced something, that was the most likely place to find it.

He said, "Dad, you don't understand. I know *where* I am—I just don't know *who* I am!"

We were ready for that one.

"Son, you were born John Wilford Grossly (name changed to protect the guilty) and as far as your mother and I know, it's never been changed!" Simple.

If I'd had the urge to tell my parents that I couldn't find myself, my mother would have looked at me and said, "What's the matter with you? If you want to find yourself, just lower your chin to your chest and look down. Lo and behold, you'll find yourself every time. . . . Go get the vacuum and get to work!"

Who I was, where I was, and where I came from were never a problem for me when I was growing up. Thanks to my daddy, I always knew where I came from and just about any other "W" you could think of.

When I walked out the door to go somewhere, Daddy always called out, "Remember who you are, to whom you belong, and where you came from— and be sure you get back here on time." He wasn't exactly reminding me of my street address or what to do in case of an accident.

We knew we mattered to Momma and Daddy, knew they felt responsible for us. They believed we were on loan to them from God, and if we got mis-

placed for long, they'd have some explaining to do—
to say nothing of the explaining we'd have to do.
Many's the time I would have rather faced the good
Lord Himself than my daddy! (We felt it was our job
to help Momma get exercise by walking the floor.)

We knew that if any of the four of us lost ourselves, Momma and Daddy would come looking for
us, find us, and remind us exactly who we were.
Then they'd take us back where we came from, home
to face the music—and it wouldn't be the fox trot.

Sometimes we thought our parents were put on
this earth to make us miserable and were succeeding
very well, but we never had any confusion about who
we were. My parents had four little Harneys to teach
who they were and where they came from. Whatever
they did must have worked because I called my
brother Jim one day and asked, "Who is this?"

He said, "It's Jim Harney. Who do you think it
is?"

Then I asked him where he came from and he
said, "I came down from the attic where I was putting up sheetrock."

Well, he knows exactly who he is but has forgotten all he ever knew about where he came from.
That's why I call him now and then—to remind him.
Brothers grow up and get distracted by their wives
and children.

I will *never* be able to forget who I am or where I
came from because at family reunions people come
up to me and *tell* me who I am. It doesn't matter how
old I am—and I've been out of diapers and walking
for quite awhile now. It doesn't matter. The same
thing always happens to me.

A person related to me by three generations removed—but still hangin' around—will walk up, grab
my cheek, and tell me exactly who I am. They say, "I
know you—you're that James Harney's daughter" or
"Why, you're that cute little Deaurelle Grigsby's little
girl" (as if my mother is still eighteen, and I'm three
and one-half months old). So as long as you have a
family reunion to attend once in a while, you will
never be able to forget who you are or where you
came from.

If you happen to be the parent of someone who
wants to go off to find himself, the only thing I know
is you don't finance it for them. If children are going
to wander around not knowing who they are, they
should do it on their own money. They're more
likely to have a short trip that way. They may suddenly remember where they came from and get back
there as fast as their billfolds run dry.

Who are we kidding? The only people who can
forget who they are and where they came from have
amnesia.

A person can travel to the four corners of the
earth trying to discover who he is, and some part of
that journey will always lead back to where he came
from—home.

He might feel like a different person, may be
older and hopefully wiser, but he'll never be enlightened until he embraces his roots, accepts the best of
them, learns from the worst of them, and goes forward from there.

If you happen to be the parent of an adult child
who is determined to wander off in search of new

horizons, you are coming face to face with the most difficult task you will ever have—that of letting go.

Myth: A Good Parent Never Lets Go

You may think the toughest thing you will ever let go of is your money. Nope! If you're a father, you may think that the toughest thing you could have to give up is Monday night football. No way!

You may think the toughest thing you'll ever have to give up is your youth. Not even close.

Maybe you think the toughest thing you'll ever have to give up is a few pounds or ice cream or chocolate or spare ribs. Nope, those are a piece of cake.

I'm no sociologist, no psychologist; I don't have a degree in statistics, musicology, or ergonomics. And as the old feller says, "I don't know much. But I do know this: The toughest job a parent has is knowing when to 'let go' and then actually doing it."

A family is a bunch of people. Some of them live with you; some of them don't. For that you may even be grateful. I know I am!

My own mother liked living with me when I was growing up. . . . Well, she liked it most of the time. But she wouldn't be crazy about living with me now. I can tell you that.

My parents saw it as their God-given job to live with us until we were grown. They felt you shouldn't give unfinished jobs back to God. Not that God can't finish the task. He's in the business of finishing what He begins. He does it all the time, but He expects us to do the same.

The actual truth is that good parents learn when to let go. They never let go too soon. Figuring out the difference is why parents cry in their sleep. There may be a few little clues to help us. For instance, good parents shouldn't expect children to act like adults, and they shouldn't appreciate it when adults act like children.

In case that failed to help, consider this. When a "child" living under your roof and eating at your table no longer wishes to accept the limited freedom within the family for the mutual good of the family—if the "child" is at least ten years past puberty, old enough to vote and keep hours that could destroy the sleep cycle of a mongoose, it's probably past time to let go.

When you let go, you say, "This is it. They're out of my hands; there's nothing more I know to do; they belong to you, God." And you let them go. When you do this, you've just placed your child in the only hands big enough to complete the job.

A hidden misunderstanding surrounds this particular myth. It is that when you decide it is time to let go—to let this adult child spend time discovering the cost of beans and motor oil—you have given up. No! You haven't given up at all. It's simply that your parenting has taken a sharp turn. This is when you really understand what it means to wear out your knees praying. This is where you should be spending more time after a child backs blindfolded into the world. You pray because you know the child is really not ready, but you know you have done all you know to do, except pray.

So you never give up, never stop praying, never stop loving. You just . . . let them go.

A Tiny Parable for Parents Only

One spring afternoon walking into the house, I happened to look down at just the right moment. There, sitting just two inches from a rock stepping stone in my back yard, was a tiny bird. He was not even two inches long if I stretched him a bit. I stopped dead in my tracks and peered down into his little eyes.

I could tell he was scared to death, but he just kept sitting there. I began to talk to him. "So, little one, did you dive out of the nest too soon, or did Momma come home today and tell you it was 'time'?" He just blinked. Then, I glanced up into the nearby trees, and there she was . . . Momma Bird. She was watching me like a hawk and didn't look one bit happy. I felt sorry for her. It was the first time in my life and probably the last that I will be on the same wavelength with a bird.

She'd done all she could for this little fella on the ground, except watch. She couldn't swoop down, grab him by the fuzz on his neck, and drag him back up into the nest. She couldn't sit down there with him and protect him from the danger of approaching feet, dogs, or cats.

She might chirp loudly once in a while, try to get his attention, but basically all she could do was watch. I'd say that if birds have the capacity for grief, she was well into it. The situation was out of her fine-feathered hands.

Later, I went out to check on the little fella and couldn't find him anywhere. Tender-hearted as I am, I am going to believe that somehow after I left him, that bird stood up on his scraggly little bird legs and began to flap his fuzzy wings as if his life depended on it. I'm going to believe that he miraculously took his first solo flight, flapped his way to safety, and is presently soaring like an eagle.

You want to know something? My husband and I have the same hope for your children—and our own children who are out in the world. They are never out of your heart; they're just out of your hands.

Myth: I Can Do
What I Want—I Live Here

My dad loves to tell the story of two men. One walks up to the other and punches him in the nose. The surprised man with the throbbing nose says, "Now, why in the world did you do that?"

The man doing the punching says, "I'm just exercising my freedom."

Then the fellow with the red nose says, "Well, there's something you should know about freedom. Your freedom ends where my nose begins."

It's like that in a family. Somebody's freedom is always extending over into another person's freedom. That's why one of the least-liked jobs of parenting is that of referee, jury, and judge. This is why many years after children leave home, a parent's brain tends to slow down a bit. It's worn out from controlling all that freedom.

My hairdresser is always full of information I never ask for, but I figure I'm paying for it, so I listen.

At one point, she was trying to rear a thirteen-year-old boy and wasn't enjoying it much. They were seeking the advice of a local child psychiatrist. He suggested she change the way she talked to the boy. He said you should never use the word *responsibility* with teenagers because they aren't equipped to handle it. (She paid good money for this advice.) Most of us already knew that not all children are equipped to handle responsibility; we just didn't realize it had anything to do with the word.

The child therapist suggested that the word *job* be substituted for the word *responsibility.*

When I heard this, I wondered what age a child should be before it's safe to expose him to the "big R word."

The child therapist suggested my hairdresser use the word *job* in place of the big R word. When I think of the word *job,* I think of getting paid for doing something. Can you imagine having enough money to pay a child to learn kindness, respect for others, patience, accountability for actions, and all those other qualities necessary for successful living?

Later on this bit of information about the word *job* came in handy for me in a backhanded sort of way. One of our sons was just about to make a career out of coming home long after his curfew. On one such occasion, I lost control. I said, "Look here, son! It's our job to tell you when to go home, and it's your job to be here—and one of us is about to be fired!"

Now, you just think about that. It sounded brilliant for about a second and a half. You tell me how you fire a teenager. Teenagers don't mind if you fire them. Where else can they go to find another "job" where all they have to do is forget to feed the dog, talk on the phone for free, and look in the refrigerator every half hour.

That's when I knew that the word *job* didn't come anywhere close to representing all we wanted to teach this young person—didn't come close to teaching personal accountability or any of those other 'bilities.

That night was the beginning of many late-night talks about responsibility versus freedom and freedom *with* responsibility. True freedom acknowledges and respects the fact that our behavior affects everyone around us and that we are always accountable for our actions. That way no one will ever be guilty of saying or even thinking, "I can do anything I want—I live here."

Myth: That the "Newest" Commandment Is Optional

The "newest" commandment has been around for a long, long time. It goes like this: "A new commandment I give to you, that you love one another; as I have loved you that you also love one another. By this love all will know that you are my disciples if you have love for one another" (John 13:34–35).

That's the "newest" commandment. So why is it we live as if this one doesn't apply in our families? We often live as if it doesn't apply at all. We live more as if it is an option to be exercised on a good day, if the wind isn't blowing and the pollen count is down.

We often live like the two little brothers who were fighting. One of them wopped the other in the face with his hand. When their mother separated them, she said to the one doing the wopping, "Now you just go in there and apologize to your brother and tell him you love him."

When the little boy returned, his mother said, "Did you apologize?"

"Yes, Ma'am."

"Did you tell him you love him?"

"No, Ma'am. He's my brother—I don't *have* to love him."

That's where the "newest" commandment comes into the picture.

And that's where we begin to go awry. Like the little boy, we suffer from the delusion that we don't have to love our families. There is a television situation comedy that deals with the ups and downs of family life. These people treat each other with all the respect you'd have for a bag of dog food.

A thirty-two-year-old woman told the story of how she was separated from a sister and brother when she was fifteen years old. Their mother died, and the younger sister and brother were placed in an adoptive home. The older sister was sent to live with her father in another state.

Seventeen years passed, and she never stopped longing for her half-brother and sister. She searched all those years trying to connect the pieces of her life. Her search ended on a national television program when the three of them were at last tearfully, joyfully reunited. They embraced as only those can who have long remembered, long desired, and finally found each other.

The older sister said, "A part of my heart has been missing all these years. . . . Now I have it back." In finding each other, they found an important part of themselves.

Some people never lose their families; they just decide to get along without them. Choosing not to get along with your family is like deciding you don't like your left leg and can get along without it. You'll find out that you can get along without it; you can even go from place to place and learn to walk again—but your life will never be the same. Something will always be missing.

The well-known actor James Earl Jones grew up without knowing his father. He recalls that as a young adult he knew that his father was a stage actor, but the two had not met. He described the deep longing to know this man who was a mysterious part of himself. One day, he turned on his television and there before his eyes was his father in a play. As he watched his dad, his entire body filled with excitement. He kept thinking, "That's *my* father! *My* father!"

Later James Earl Jones was able to locate his father's address, called him, and set up a day to meet him. He couldn't wait for the appointed day and went to his father's residence unexpectedly.

He found his dad working in the yard. When James Earl Jones saw his dad in the flesh for the first time he thought, *My goodness . . . he's so tall!* The two men embraced and began a new lifetime association as friends. James Earl Jones said, "There's no way to make up for twenty-five lost years. You can only begin a relationship as friends and go forward from there." The two remain close to this day.

So how is it that so many willingly walk away from family, and others spend their lives searching for them.

If you're waiting for your family to be perfect, you'd better get in line and bring a large lunch as the saying goes. You'll be there a long, long time. Most of our families couldn't get close to perfect if you put them on a Federal Express plane and pointed it in the right direction.

I've been blessed to know quite a few wonderful families, but not one of them is perfect. Families are made up of people like you and me, and we are imperfect people learning, growing, doing the best we can. But in my observation of families I do have an idea about those who come as close to perfect as is humanly possible. They are those who continue to look for ways to understand each other. They are people who make the choice to love each other, flaws and all. They are people who realize that by loving family they are loving part of themselves. They are people who know that God's love is to be lived out within the walls of our homes . . . and out into the world from there.

While attending a mother-daughter banquet recently, I was blessed to experience a mother and daughter who had been asked to write letters to each other and share them with the group. The letters touched me, and I asked their permission to use por-

tions of the daughter's letter, as it expressed so many
of the important qualities of family.

The daughter writes:

> Mom, I'm glad I have the opportunity to do this. I
> have been fortunate to grow up in a home where
> we, all of us, can openly show our love for each
> other. So I'm not writing this letter because I can't
> "say" I love you. I can, and I say it often. But I
> never take those words lightly. However, some
> words don't get said often enough—words like, "I
> admire you, respect you, and hope to be like you."
>
> When our pastor preached his sermon on godly
> mothers, you fit the description completely. Thank
> you for loving me enough to love Jesus. Mom,
> thank you for your prayers. I know you pray for
> each of us daily. There's just something about a
> mother's prayers.
>
> I look back at all the times you've been my mom
> and my friend. If I were to write them all, they
> would fill volumes of books. I remember the day
> in tenth grade when my boyfriend and I broke up.
> I called you from school crying, and you said
> you'd be "right there." You came from work and
> took me shopping! You know the right things to
> do and say! Thank you for listening to all my prob-
> lems; you are the *best* listener!
>
> And thank you for the times when the last thing
> I wanted to do was laugh, and you wouldn't give
> up until I was smiling. Thank you for all the times
> you started dancing to the tune on the radio—that
> made me laugh every time!
>
> I love you, and someday I hope my daughter (if
> I ever get married) will be able to say she thinks of
> me as a friend. Thank you, Mom.
>
> With deep love, admiration, and affection,
>
>   Your only daughter

We'd all live in a better world if everyone left this sort of legacy for their children. When you are related to a bunch of people by birth or simply, most importantly, "only" by love, you should perceive yourself as truly blessed.

ABOUT THE AUTHOR

Sylvia Harney, the eldest of four children of a Baptist minister, grew up living in several small middle Tennessee towns. This environment became fertile ground for the stories contained in her books. Her father's great love for people and her mother's sense of humor and love of laughter have been passed on to Sylvia.

Sylvia graduated from Belmont College with a degree in Education. She is married to commercial photographer Hank Widick and resides in Franklin, Tennessee with their black labrador retriever named Gracie.

She now travels extensively, speaking to various conventions, churches, and women's groups across America. With the publication of her first book, *Married Beyond Recognition* (Wolgemuth & Hyatt, 1988), Sylvia established herself as a writer who could create humor that tugs at the heart strings.

Every Time I Go Home I Break Out in Relatives continues to celebrate her love of family and of memories both old and new. Sylvia may be contacted through Ambassador Speakers Bureau, P.O. Box 50358, Nashville, Tennessee, 37024.

The typeface for the text of this book is *Palatino*. This type—best known as a contemporary *italic* typeface—was a post-World War II design crafted by the talented young German calligrapher Hermann Zapf. For inspiration, Zapf drew upon the writing legacy of a group of Italian Renaissance writing masters, in which the typeface's namesake, Giovanni Battista Palatino, was numbered. Giovanni Palatino's *Libro nuovo d'imparare a scrivera* was published in Rome in 1540 and became one of the most used, wide-ranging writing manuals of the sixteenth century. Zapf was an apt student of the European masters, and contemporary *Palatino* is one of his contributions to modern typography.

Substantive Editing:
Stephen Hines

Copy Editing:
Donna Sherwood

Cover Design:
Steve Diggs & Friends
Nashville, Tennessee

Page Composition:
Xerox Ventura Publisher
Printware 720 IQ Laser Printer

Printing and Binding:
Maple-Vail Printing Group
York, Pennsylvania

Cover Printing:
Strine Printing Company
York, Pennsylvania